Hoodoo
Return and
Reconciliation
Spells

TRUE LOVE MAGIC
IN THE CONJURE TRADITION

BY DEACON MILLETT

Lucky Mojo Curio Company
Forestville, California

⇨ 2015 ⇦

Hoodoo Return and Reconciliation Spells:
True Love Magic in the Conjure Tradition
by Deacon Millett
FourAltars.org

Text:
Deacon Millett

Editor:
catherine yronwode

Cover:
Greywolf C. Townsend, Charles C. Dawson

production:
nagasiva yronwode, catherine yronwode, Greywolf Townsend

Illustrations:
Charles C. Dawson, R. C. Adams, P. Craig Russell, Nelson C. Hahne,
Pamela Colman Smith, Greywolf C. Townsend, Leslie Cabarga, Joseph E. Meyer,
Deacon Millett, catherine yronwode, Charlie Wylie, Unknown Sovereign Artist.

Some material in this book appeared at the
Lucky Mojo Curio Company Forum
Forum.LuckyMojo.com
Used With Permission

First Edition 2015 / Second Edition 2017

Published by
The Lucky Mojo Curio Company
6632 Covey Road
Forestville, California 95436
LuckyMojo.com

ISBN: 978-0-9719612-9-6

Printed in Canada.

Contents

Dedication 4

Acknowledgements 4

The Situation

    Lovesick and Heartbroken 5

    Return, Reconnect, Reunite, Reconcile 6

    The Voices of Experience 7

    Rules of the Road 10

    When Is It Really "Too Late"? 11

The Spells

    Who Do You Love? 12

    Newbell Niles Puckett 13

    Helen Pitkin: "An Angel by Brevet" 14

    The Fabled Black Cat Bone 15

    Pictures, Papers, and Proxies 17

    Tumba Walla, Bumba Walla, Return to Me 24

    H.U. Lampe's Famous Spells 26

    Star Crossed Lovers 27

    Love Uncrossing 28

    Averting the Evil Eye 29

    Hoodoo Bible Magic 30

    How to Make Him Think of You 33

    Forgive and Forget 34

    Reconciliation Baths 36

    Love Letters Straight from Your Heart 38

    Alive with Magnetism! 42

    Please, Saint Anthony, Look Around 45

    Heart Lights and Love Lamps 46

    Signs of Love 52

    Tarot Cards in Love Readings 54

    Personal Concerns to Aid the Lovelorn 56

    When There Are No Personal Concerns 58

    Overcoming a Mother's Manipulation 59

    Love Spells from the Drug Store 60

    The Life and Works of Marie Laveau 62

    3-Ace-Queen-7 Return to Me 67

    Miss Cat's Down-Home Short-and-Simples 68

    Lover, Come Back to Me 69

    Graveyard Love 73

    Stay with Me 74

Frequently Asked Questions 75

Dedication

To Dr. E., Ekun dayo oni Shangó, and Rev. Hyperion
Thank you for bringing love to so many, Eddy. We miss you.

Acknowledgements

Catherine Yronwode has been my comrade-in-arms for years — and the very first thing she did when we met was patiently listen as I poured out my love woes. I pray that each of you may be blessed with such a friend's compassionate ear, discerning eye, and wise counsel.

Matthew Pavesic makes every day of my life happier, easier, or more adventurous — and that can't be easy! I pray each of you may be blessed with companionship, acceptance, and someone always on your side!

The wonderful members of the Lucky Mojo Forum (Hi, AnaP and justa!) have honest hearts, questing minds, and gentle souls, and the Forum Moderators dish out love, caring, and hoodoo advice every day. I pray that each of you may be blessed with such belonging!

Forestville, California, is my home away from home. Thank you, Nagasiva, Susie, Don, Diana, Robin, Heidi, Alicia, Eileen — all the Lucky Mojo Curio Co. staff, past, present, and future! I pray that all who read this find as warm a welcome at some place in their lives.

Between the three of them, the folklorists Newbell Niles Puckett, Zora Neale Hurston, and Reverend Harry Middleton Hyatt interviewed more than 2,000 Black American hoodoo rootworkers during the middle 50 years of the 20th century, for which my gratitude is freely given. Thanks and respect are also owed to the practitioners and professional spiritual workers who shared their foundational love spells with the folklorists.

Many further contributions herein were provided by my colleagues from the Association of Independent Readers and Rootworkers:

Catherine Yronwode	Ms. Melanie	Miss Bri
Devi Spring	Lukianos	Khi Armand
Professor Porterfield	Dr. Johannes	ConjureMan Ali
Miss Michaele	Dr. E.	Miss Aida

I am lucky to be a part of this Missionary Independent Spiritual Church outreach. Thank you all for your continued love and support.

Lovesick and Heartbroken

Inevitably, we turn to hoodoo when something is *wrong*, when there is a problem we cannot solve. The earliest accounts of conjure show a definite bias for health and protection spells to make things easier for slaves and servants. But a current of love work was ever-present, and after Emancipation, love and prosperity took center stage among the spells.

The feelings love evokes are potent — and beyond our control. When a loved one leaves us, we are left feeling barren, destitute, panic-stricken.

This is how I came to hoodoo, and it may well be why you picked up this book. You will get through this. Just about every human has, at one time or another. Which doesn't make it any better.

Here are some of the symptoms you may be feeling: loss of appetite, sleeplessness, inability to concentrate, obsessive thoughts, panic attacks, anger, and denial. This is not a good space in which to begin a serious spiritual work, yet time is of the essence, for with each passing day your loved one moves farther away.

Take a deep breath. Self-cleansing and calming are paramount, because desperation can ruin any return to me work you embark upon. I use a powerful blend of Lucky Mojo brand Clarity, Tranquility, and Van Van Oils on white vigil candles to steady the nerves and calm the mind. The same blend is perfect to dot the forehead, temples, heart, and wrists.

Nature is powerfully grounding, and actually hugging a tree can lend you its strength. Remember, negative and obsessive thoughts cannot be willed away! They must be *replaced* with something. A twenty minute walk in the sun while reciting the Serenity Prayer will help immensely:

> *God, grant me the Serenity*
> *to accept the things I cannot change,*
> *Courage to change the things I can,*
> *and the Wisdom to know the difference.*

A BLUE BATH TO REMOVE NEGATIVE ENERGY

Aura LaForest recommends this bath for those experiencing a deep feeling of sadness. Dissolve a square of Reckitts' Crown Blue or a Blue Anil Ball in a pot of very hot water. Add 1 teaspoon lemon juice and a few drops of Van Van Oil. Dilute into a bathtub of warm water for bathing.

Return, Reconnect, Reunite, Reconcile

Love work comes in two basic flavours: *Attraction* and *Reconciliation*. One is about new love, whether we have a specific person in mind or not. The other is about old love, rekindling it and mending its flaws. Sweetening, the subject of my previous book, *Hoodoo Honey and Sugar Spells,* is useful in both attraction and reconciliation work — whether we've found someone we want to make sweet on us or need to sweeten an existing relationship gone sour.

The umbrella term *reconciliation* encompasses many different aims:

Do we want an ex-boyfriend or girlfriend to *return* to us? If so, we may wish to do some form of spell involving movement, such as bringing two candles closer and closer together. Geographic distance, real or symbolic, is what we're facing here.

Do we wish to *reconnect* to a long lost love or a recent flame who is refusing our calls? A communication job may be our best bet, perhaps a love letter fixed with Love Me Sachet Powder.

Do we desire to *reunite* with someone we desperately miss, perhaps from long ago? A working in which two disparate elements join together would suit such a situation perfectly, helping bridge the gap made by time.

Or do we actually want to *reconcile* — and if so, what exactly does that word mean? A lot of things, it turns out. To reconcile is:

- to cause to become amicable, as when we reconcile enemy factions.
- to make compatible, such as reconciling fiscal accounts.
- to settle a dispute, or reconcile a disagreement.
- to restore to good standing in a church, such as the Catholic sacrament of reconciliation (known more familiarly as confession).
- to bring into agreement or harmony, when we reconcile differing points of view or eyewitness testimonies.
- and, lastly, to be resigned to something not desired, as when we are reconciled to our fate.

I'm not sure we could find a more fitting word than *reconciliation* for this difficult work of restoring lost trust, fixing broken communication, easing anger and pain, and creating a bond of forgiveness and acceptance. In most cases, more separates us than mere geography or time. The need for some kind of reconciliation is paramount.

The Voices of Experience

This is a book filled with return and reconciliation spells for the home practitioner, works that you can do all on your own to bring back love and move forward as a couple. However, you don't have to go it all on your own. In addition to listening to the many voices of rootworkers from the past whose spells are included here, you can hire your own spiritual worker to provide readings, magical coaching or rootwork consultations, or to cast spells in tandem with you, to back up the work.

Now, to be honest, not all rootworkers will take on every case, and the good, ethical, and successful ones often set limits on how they work for clients. Here, in their own words, are some of the best workers currently in practice, with honest, straightforward advice for you:

MIS BRI: LISTEN FOR THE DIVINE ANSWER
"Reconciliation is a process that is affected by time and frequency of communication between yourself and your partner — the longer you have been apart and the less communication there has been, the harder the case is to resolve. Even in cases where we try to do everything correctly, the Divine answer is still sometimes no — a good worker and a good client will pay heed to that and move forward accordingly."

CONJUREMAN ALI: REPAIR THE RIFT
"I am actually of the mind that reconciliation is no harder than any other work that we do. The only difficulty comes from the people themselves. Magically the work is the same, but it is up to the people involved to take advantage of the opportunities that Spirit provides. Not everyone is willing to forgive and work together to repair the rift. This is where the failures in reconciliation occur. I set realistic expectations, but I think the idea that reconciliation is a long-shot is not one I personally agree with. If this was the case, I wouldn't do this work."

JOSEPH MAGNUSON: DON'T WAIT TOO LONG
"The further apart the people are and the further in the past the relationship gets, the more distant the connectors get. New people and new factors come into their lives. As a worker, I prefer fresh cases, and people who are okay with putting a time limit on reconciliation work."

MAMA MIKI: CAN YOU LET GO OF THE PAST?

"Many factors contribute to the success or failure of spell work, including the skill of the practitioner; the strength of the target to resist; the proper use of herbs, oils, or candles; outside interfering influences; and ultimately, God's will. Reconciliation can also be difficult for some clients because it requires that both parties change their attitudes and let go of the past. The more time passes, the less chance there is that they can do so. Before hiring help, consider if it is worth your time, money, and energy to get your ex back. There may be someone out there who is better for you."

DR. JOHANNES: CURING AND MENDING

"Begin by questioning the belief that doctor + pharmacy = cure.

"A common cold provides a good analogy:. Some people are cured by a placebo, some are cured by Elderberries, some by Eucalyptus, some by Sampson Snake Root. Some common colds turn into pneumonia and require penicillin. Some people seem to carry a simple cold for years and no medicine will work; then it turns out that they are allergic and the right cure is finally found. And some people die from simple colds.

"This is not very different from reconciliations. In some cases it just requires that two people talk to each other again, in some cases a bit more, and in some cases the problem is so bad that no cure can fix this.

"What do I mean by "no cure"? Well, for example, let's say that a heterosexual couple broke up because one of them came out as gay, but the other one denies this and wants the ex back; there is no cure. Another example: The person who wants the ex back used to abuse the ex, who then ran away; again, there is no cure, or very little chance of one.

"When it comes to difficult reconciliations, if a cure is possible, then patience and continuous work over a pre-determined time frame are two major factors in achieving success. Compare this to the naive formula of doctor + pharmacy = cure and you will see that spiritual rootwork is similarly as complex as medicine.

"To use another analogy, hiring rootworker after rootworker for a reconciliation is a bit like handing over a broken vase. The job of the practitioner is to try and patch it back together, make sure it looks good and stays water proof. The more shattered the vase is, the longer it may take to patch it together. Such spiritual repair work requires more patience than merely getting something new to put flowers into."

CATHERINE YRONWODE: NO TIMELINE, NO CASE

"Every worker is different. Some are more gifted for, and spiritually more drawn to, performing reconciliation work than others. You can't expect a baseball player to excel at football. Choose your worker well.

"Every case is different. There is no 'one size fits all' rule in reconciliation and some cases are more likely to succeed than others. You can't make a silk purse out of a sow's ear. Some attempts fail because the situation prior to the break-up was bad.

"Every case has its own timeline. Clients always ask me, "How long will it take?" The answer is that this will vary from case to case.

"The shortest reconciliation case i ever took was solved when the man phoned and asked to come over *while i was on the phone with the client* giving her instructions on how to answer the phone when he called! (She had been under the false impression, which she had picked up via bad internet spell advice, that she should 'show him a cold shoulder when he calls, until he *begs* for her' — really bad advice!).

"The longest reconciliation case i have taken to date lasted *six years* after the woman was literally stood up at the altar on her wedding day. Yes, she eventually got her man — and her wedding. However, this client saw steady progress along the way and we performed check-readings on a regularly scheduled basis for the entire six years. It took less than a year for the man to resume sex with her; within the next year they were living together, and then all we had to do was work on emotionally freeing him from the enmeshing clutches of his extremely obstructive ex-wife and adult children for the next four years. Was it a 'long shot'? Yes and no. The man had bolted completely — but, previously to bolting, he *had* planned a wedding, so it was not as if we had to give him a complete reality-transplant; we just had to work by stages as we re-focussed him back to sexual pleasure, back to emotional intimacy, back to shared financial links, and then back to the altar!

"Every client should be willing to set a timeline for specific partial goals (resumption of sex, living together, marriage) before engaging the services of a professional root doctor. If the client has no specific goals for fulfilment of the timeline, either in stages or in whole, the worker should not take the case. Extracting a timeline from my reconciliation clients is often extremely difficult, and uninformed clients often ask me to go at the job in an open-ended way. But 'no timeline, no case.' That's my rule."

Rules of the Road

If you've had a break-up and wish to reunite or reconcile, you are in a vulnerable position. There are several rules of the road to help you if you move forward with spellwork.

- **Beware of Extravagant Promises by Online Spell-Casters:** "Guaranteed Results" are a guaranteed scam. Don't believe anyone who promises to "re-unite lovers in 24 hours." If you are too heart-broken to trust your own rootwork, find an authentic conjure doctor who prescribes baths or candle spells you can do to back up the work.
- **Get a Reading:** A psychic reading may help you gain added perspective — if you let it. "If the person is not right for you, a reading will reveal this," says rootworker Catherine Yronwode. "It may also reveal that spells will not heal a cycle of incompatibility, but will merely extend your time until the next fight or break-up, and the next, and the next — until you finally wise up and look for a new, more compatible partner." An ethical worker is entirely justified in turning down a hopeless reconciliation or return case — for your own good!
- **Know Your Odds:** Ask your reader what the outlook is that reunion can occur, and then weigh that carefully against any investment in time and money you are contemplating.
- **Don't Cross Up Your Own Work:** If you are wearing love oils and working a sugar spell, don't send the Intranquil Spirit after your ex to torment him. If you have burned a candle on his name and he suddenly phones, do pick up the call — and don't start a fight.
- **Give the Work a Time Limit:** Set a date for when you will give up — and then stick to it. Yronwode has a wonderful method for this: Light a white candle, and dress it with Psychic Vision Oil, 7-11 Holy Oil, or anything soothing. While it is burning, sit quietly in meditation. When you are completely calm, ask: "How long, Lord, should I work to get this man back?" An answer will be given to you: "One year," "Until my birthday," "January 1st." That is your date. Say it out loud and affirm it. "I want you to know the date and time that this work will be finished, Yronwode says, "and to stick with it, whether the spell succeeds or fails. This is the best way I know to help a person who is 'stuck' in lost-love work."

When Is It Really "Too Late"?

Reconciliation work is described as a "long shot" by her reader, yet the desperate client convinces herself that "the reader said we had a chance of getting back together." Surrounded by ads that promise "Lovers Re-United — 24 Hours — Guaranteed!" she throws money at fraudulent spell-casters, but is asked to send no personal concerns, and hence no actual conjure work is done.

A month or two after the break-up, she finally starts a "traditional" hoodoo sugar jar. Nothing happens. Turns out the jar is not so traditional after all — the internet instructions tell her to put Domination Oil and Cayenne Pepper in the sugar, fill it with tap water, and put the jar in the freezer "to freeze him in place so he can't run away."

Back on the net, she learns a new spell that teaches her how to send a vicious, damned spirit after her ex and at the same time to ignore all of his phone calls and texts until he "begs for forgiveness." So when he calls, she doesn't pick up the phone. Eventually, he hooks up with someone else. She counts it as a victory because he hasn't yet blocked her on Facebook.

Finally she calls a real rootworker. She describes the $12,000.00 she spent on the fake spell-caster, the freezer spell, and the evil spirit in her bedroom, and she wants the rootworker to fix it all with a $7.00 bottle of oil and two pink candles. The rootworker says he can't, because "the case is now lost." The client objects, "but my reader said it was a possibility!"

So she buys this book. But the spells are all so ... simple. There are no demons, no magic wands, no pointy-hatted witches. Instead, it's al about photos, foot tracks, socks, and sugar. The spells are so "easy" ... but ...

She doesn't have a couple-photo because "We never actually dated."

She doesn't have a hair because "I never believed in this stuff before."

She doesn't have his underwear because "I threw all his stuff away."

If this page describes you — and it will probably only be true of about five percent of the people reading it — then I want you to take a moment to contemplate what went wrong, and resolve to do better next time. Make wiser choices, be more alert to signs, start working with personal concerns earlier, and about all, keep love in your heart.

Your rootworker was right: It's too late for this case.

The good news is that you *can* love again.

In the meantime, pass this book along to someone who can use it.

Who Do You Love?

From Bo Diddley's "Who Do You Love?" to Clarence Thomas's "Who put pubic hair on my Coke?" hoodoo hides just beneath the surface of American consciousness. On the campaign trail, Barack Obama's pockets were full of lucky charms, and a TSA airport screener recently gestured to my red flannel mojo hand with a knowing look (and keeping his hands *off!*).

To the public at large, the words **hoodoo, mojo,** and **Voodoo** are simply generic terms for the ineffable, referenced by luminaries from Austin Powers to George H. W. Bush. I believe a lot of this is due to White folks hearing blues music and using context to come up with pseudo-meanings, inaccurate but with a certain kind of (non)sense.

In this book, we are more specific:

Hoodoo, also known as conjure, rootwork, tricking, and using that stuff, is an African-American system of folk magic that developed during the collision between African religious magic and Christianity.

Mojos are wrapped bundles of spiritual elements used for love, luck, uncrossing, and protection. They have many other names, including hands, tobies, jomos, trick bags, conjure bags, and gris-gris. The last-named is the French spelling of gri-gri or gree-gree, an African word for a charm bag.

Voodoo or **Vodou,** an African religion of Haiti, is mischaracterized in popular American culture as a hodgepodge of "savage" dancing, White Zombies, Voodoo Queens, and pin-pricked poppets. However, in the very first sentence of 1931's "Hoodoo In America," the Black folklorist Zora Neale Hurston got straight to the point: "Veaudeau is the European term for African magic practices and beliefs, but it is unknown to the American Negro. His own name for his practices is hoodoo."

Other cultural influences have added a touch of the exotic to hoodoo. Native American herbal lore, European grimoires, the Spiritual Church movement, Asian incenses, Pennsylvania Dutch Pow Wow magic, Jewish Psalms — all have enriched the African-American experience. It is to this tradition that I pay my respects.

In *Hoodoo Honey and Sugar Spells,* I described the work of several who came before me in this field, particularly Harry M. Hyatt, Zora Neale Hurston, and Catherine Yronwode. In this book, I will introduce you to Newbell Niles Puckett, Helen Pitkin Schertz, H. U. Lampe, and the many Black Americans who shared their spells with them — and us.

Newbell Niles Puckett

Folk Beliefs of the Southern Negro, published in 1926, is powerful in its scope, citing 400 individuals and institutions as source material, along with 280 additional references. Its author, Newbell Niles Puckett, was born and raised in Mississippi before going to Yale for graduate school, giving the data unshakeable bona fides. Also to his credit, he carefully preserved the names of his informants, so you will find them noted in this book as well.

On the down-side, Puckett's casual racism and cultural condescension make *Folk Beliefs of the Southern Negro* difficult to read in ways that Harry Hyatt's five volumes happily avoid. But better to take on such ugliness forthrightly than whitewash the past with feigned "colour blindness." Hoodoo exists in part to address this power differential between oppressor and oppressed. It is a core quality, without which conjure would be barren.

Here are two love spells, shared by Dr. H. Roger Williams of Mobile, Alabama — presented just as the ever-skeptical Puckett wrote them out.

COMMON SENSE AND FRENCH LOVE POWDER
A little common sense mixed with the charm will often bring the desired result whether the charm itself works or not. A New Orleans "hoodoo-man" sold a suitor some "French Love Powder" (sugar of milk in this case) for $5.00. He was to sprinkle this upon whatever he gave to the woman, but he was always to take her something she liked and lots of it; he was never to cross the woman nor make her mad no matter how much she annoyed him or flirted with other men; he was to show her on every occasion that he was interested in her alone. A few months later the man came back singing the praise of the conjurer, and introduced to him the woman, who, by his wonderful love-powder was induced to become his wife.

A MEDICINE TO CURE QUARRELLING
A "conjure-woman" in Algiers, Louisiana, was given $5.00 for a bottle of medicine (lemonade) to break a husband of quarrelling. Her directions were for the unhappy wife to fill her mouth with the medicine whenever her good man began to quarrel and not to swallow it until he had ceased. Then she was to swallow the medicine and kiss him. So successful was this treatment that several wives came to the doctor upon recommendation for the same prescription.

Helen Pitkin: An Angel by Brevet

An Angel by Brevet: A Story of Modern New Orleans was published in 1904 and twenty years later, Helen Pitkin's novel was used by Puckett as source material. There is some great spell work embedded in this story.

Angelique, the heroine, has a love-rival and visits Madame Peggy for aid.

"Angele now suffered the most strenuous embarrassment she had ever known. 'I love where I am not loved in return,' she said in a hard voice."

She is asked to remove all her black clothing. "Nothing must be crossed, neither your feet, neither your hands. For fear two pins might cross in your hair, it is best to take them out now."

An altar of fruit, candies, and alcohol is on the floor.

"In the centre a saucer was set, in which were white sand, quicksilver, and molasses, apexed by a blue candle ... On the hearth [was] a large black pot, from which there was the whisper of a simmer and a luscious steam."

In the ceremony that follows, we see hoodoo touches: Angele must write her own name, her lover's, and her rival's on slips of paper. The slip with her rival's name is placed to soak in a dish of vinegar, salt, and Pepper; the name papers of herself and her beloved are dropped into a bowl of burning whiskey "that sent leaping shadows into the dark corners.

"Ma'm Peggy lifted the candles from the altar ... and handed one to Angele. It bore seven notches in the blue tallow, and Ma'm Peggy instructed her to burn it seven nights in her own bedroom, only from notch to notch, repeating three Hail Mary's. The sorceress then gave Angele a pinch of the poiv' guine [Guinea Grains] from the saucer and bade her put five grains in her mouth whenever her lover would come near her, this to soften him towards her; also, when he would first enter the house, to make a glass of sugared water, very sweet, and with basilique [Basil], and throw it in the yard with her back towards the street."

Put Guinea Grains and Cloves in your mouth, and you can get anything you want from your White man, Ma'm Peggy tells her, before also teaching that Lodestone can "ambition a man." Basil is used for a happy home.

Helen Pitkin Schertz (1877-1945) was a newspaper journalist as well as a poet and novelist. Puckett trusted her accounts, affirming that "Although written in the form of fiction, [Pitkin] assures me, personally, that they are scientifically accurate, being an exact reproduction of what she herself has seen or obtained from her servants and absolutely free from imagination."

The Fabled Black Cat Bone

I believe to my soul, my baby has a black cat bone,
Every time I leave her, sure that I'll go back home.
— Andrew "Smokey" Hogg

The most famous love-returning spell in hoodoo is cruel and abusive — yet it is a strange fact that this conjure staple originates in a 19th century grimoire, *Libro de San Cipriano*, published in Spain. How it came to be so widely known in the American south is a mystery, but numerous blues songs mention the Black Cat Bone, as do dozens of Harry Hyatt's informants, and Puckett noted that "I will use my black-cat bone," was a well-known comment made by a jealous lover to a rival.

"While the chief power of such a bone is that of making a person invisible, it will also enable you to marry your choice (Mary Robinson, Calhoun, Alabama, and L. Wiggins, Fort Valley, Georgia), will bring you good luck all your life (Southland Institute, Southland, Arkansas), and, in fact, some say, will fix you so that you can do anything whatsoever (Cleo Jefferson, Fort Valley, Georgia)."

"If you get a black cat's bone, you can travel out of the sight of people and do whatever you want to do. But to get it, you must sell yourself to the Devil." That's what William Jones of Mobile, Alabama, told Zora Neale Hurston. "Catch a pure black cat alive," he said. "Put your water on and let it come to a boil and drop the cat in. He will holler three times and you must cuss him three times."

Hurston's conjure mentor Father Simms of New Orleans agreed: "You have to catch a black cat in the evening and boil him and close the lid down on the pot tightly. At twelve o'clock at night you pass every bone through your mouth till you get to the bitter bone, and that's the one."

"Put the bone in your mouth," Jones said, "and you can disappear whenever you wish. It will also fix you so the white folks will never deny you — never refuse you anything."

Puckett noted that on the Georgia Sea Islands, the bones are held up one by one before the mirror and the one that shows no reflection is lucky. Or all the bones are thrown into running water and the special bone refuses to sink. Others said the cat should be cooked in a graveyard and the bones thrown into running water; the bone that floats upstream is the proper one.

A BLACK CAT BONE AND A CANDLE ON HER PICTURE

Author, teacher, and folklorist Catherine Yronwode has studied blues lyrics for their often evocative references to hoodoo. A 1924 recording of "Hoodoo Blues," written by Spencer Williams and sung by Bessie Brown, uses the bone talisman alongside a very old-style conjure trick:

> Goin' 'neath her window, gonna lay a black cat bone
> Goin' 'neath her window, gonna lay a black cat bone
> Burn a candle on her picture, she won't let my good man alone.

"The black cat bone is for the return of the narrator's lover (he seems to have moved into another woman's home) and burning a candle (a black one, i'd wager) on her picture is to get her to let loose of the man so he can return to the singer," Yronwode says. She abhors the use of the black cat bone, but says that to "burn a candle on a picture" is "a solid work of influence that can be used for everything from boss-fixing to hot-footing and, of course, to drive off rivals or bring about return and reconciliation."

One of Hyatt's informants in New Orleans instructed him to use a glass of water, a new white saucer, a photograph, and a red candle for a controlling trick. Take the photograph and stand it upside-down, leaning it against the glass of water. Place a name paper under the saucer. On the name paper, write his name nine times, with your name nine times over it.

"See, you always got yours on top and you got him underneath you. And you put the paper under the saucer, and the water in the glass, and the picture upside-down. And you burn that candle three times a day — a red candle. You burn it at six in the morning, at twelve o'clock, six in the evening; only three times a day."

According to Yronwode, burning a candle on a photo "is still one of the most frequently mentioned spells in hoodoo and i am told or asked about it by my customers twice a month or more." She adds that, "The use of a photo marks it as a late 19th to 20th century spell, and its older form is not known to me, but i suspect that a drawing or shadow-tracing of the person was used before the invention of photography." This spell uses both the image of the target and the target's name to connect the conjure to its intended recipient.

For more on blues lyrics as a repository of conjure history, see:
LuckyMojo.com/blues.html

Pictures, Papers, and Proxies

Connecting our work to the target is a vital part of conjure. Without that connection, we may be engaged in powerful prayer, but it hardly qualifies as hoodoo. While some spells, such as a dressed letter touched by the recipient, Hot Foot Powder sprinkled on a doorstep, or an oil that you wear need to be worked directly on the target via contact or proximity, other jobs can be done at a distance. In such cases, pictures, petition papers, and proxies, especially doll babies, all connect the rootwork to its intended target.

A PICTURE IS WORTH A THOUSAND WORDS

The most important connection in this day and age is the photograph, long thought of as a "theft of the soul" in many cultures. In fact, the Kayapo people of the Brazilian Amazon have a phrase "akaron kaba," which means both "to take a photo" and "to steal a soul." If you've ever watched a Polaroid photo develop (and shaken it ritualistically to "help" the process along), you've experienced the amazement a captured image can evoke.

In love work, a photograph of the couple concerned is best — and I am continually amazed by the people who, in this age of phone-cameras, Facebook, and selfies, cannot come up with a single photo of themselves next to their loved one. As a professional conjure workers, I spend part of every day in Photoshop, pasting people together in a modern ritual of reconciliation! Which raises an important question: If you did not have the opportunity to take a happy photograph while you were dating, just how much chance is there to bring you together once parted?

I am a big fan of putting hearts around people, or placing them in front of a background full of Roses. Cutting the photo into a heart shape and even pasting it on a paper lace heart doily are not just for February 14th! The added trouble of creating a Valentine for your love working pays generous benefits in the end.

And what of that heart symbol? It clearly has nothing to do with the pulmonary system. Instead, a shapely female buttocks is the most likely candidate, though a Rorschach test of possibilities exists, including the vulva, the testicles, the Violet or Hearts-Ease leaf, and even the Silphium seed, an ancient herbal contraceptive.

PHOTOGRAPH TO MAKE A PERSON THINK OF YOU

The Boy-Girl, a transgendered person whom Hyatt interviewed in New Orleans, Louisiana, recounted this spell to make a person think of you:

"You take the photograph and put it up. Place flowers around the photograph and burn a pink candle, bottom-side upwards." Butting the candle in this fashion by cutting the wick-end off and then sharpening the base, is common when reversing evil or, in this case, to bring back a lover.

"Write the man's name nine times with a sharp-pointed needle — nine times toward you on the candle. Then roll it in honey and sulphur, but *toward* you, and set it up and burn it. And you can command the name of the picture to do what you want to do. And when the picture is moving around the candle, the person is supposed to be thinking about you. The picture moves just like wind is shaking the picture. And when the candle burns completely down, the person will appear at your house that you desire to see."

OLIVE OIL ON PHOTOGRAPH TO BRING LOVE

A worker from Waycross, Georgia, gave Hyatt this method to bring love using a photograph:

Take the picture of your target and place nine drops of Olive Oil (Sweet Oil) around the head. Recite Psalms 23 over the photograph and carry it in your pocket. Each day, recite Psalms 23 over the photograph before putting it in your pocket. On the ninth day, your target will love you.

MIRROR AND PHOTO TO BE THE APPLE OF THEIR EYE

Madam Lindsey, a professional Spiritualist and root doctor of Algiers, Louisiana, told Hyatt this work of reconciliation:

"You get a brand-new mirror, a small ten-cent one will do. Put this person's photograph on the back, facing in. Prop the mirror so that their head is upside down. And you get a red candle and a red apple. Write this person's name on parchment seven times, and stick it down into the red apple. This is to make them think of you continually. As long as that apple is fresh, they can't forget you. Put the red candle into the hole in the apple and set it before the mirror. Whatever anger that person has for you, it'll fade away. Then you'll get to be the apple of their eye again. Do this with seven different candles. If the candle burns the apple, you'll have to get a fresh apple and a fresh parchment paper and start again."

A PHOTO, WHITE HANDKERCHIEF, AND BIBLE

"They say if someone is away and you have a photo, you place it in a white pocket handkerchief and put it in the Bible and they will come back on the ninth day." Hyatt learned this in Wilmington, North Carolina.

PHOTO, MAYFAIR POWDER, JOHN THE CONQUEROR

A New Orleans, Louisiana, informant told Hyatt how to use powdered John the Conqueror root: "You go out in some private place at 12 o'clock, when the sun is beaming hot. You walk around her picture and sprinkle it with Mayfair Powder [a brand of perfumed face powder] and John the Conqueror Root [powder]. After you do that nine times for nine days, you don't have to worry no more. She's got to come back."

A PHOTO AND THE FOUR CORNERS OF THE WORLD

In Fayetteville, North Carolina, Hyatt was told to take a photo and "nail it up, you know, in the four corners of the room. In nine days he'll be back home. Call the four corners — North, South, East, West — just like they say, 'the four corners of the world.'" The reference is to the Book of Isaiah.

A PHOTO, A GLASS OF WATER, AND A COMMAND

"Put the photograph on that glass of water, face down. After you put it on there, you stand over it and say, 'I want you to come back home. Come back! Come back! Come back!' Let it stay there for nine days and on the 10th day, that person will be back. I've seen that tried." Hyatt heard this spell in Wilmington, North Carolina.

A PHOTO OVER THE DOOR TO CALL HIM BACK

A Newport News, Virginia, worker told Hyatt, "Take a picture of a man and put it over the door. Call it three mornings, three times each morning. They tell me he'll come back. I know that's true. I know a lady did it."

A PHOTO PACKET TO BIND A LOVER TO YOU

Yronwode says that to bind a lover, place a photo of you and a photo of your love on a square of red cloth, face-to-face, with Knot Weed, Periwinkle, Rose petals, and Love Me Powder. Fold the cloth over, tie it with a shoelace from each party, dress it with Return To Me Oil, and keep it under your bed. If he has left town, bury it at your doorstep, rather than under the bed.

NAME PAPERS AND PETITIONS

Whether simple initials embraced by a heart or a more complex petition paper of overlapping names encircled with our wishes, name papers and petition papers show the primacy in hoodoo of both the written word and people's names. Many a school notebook and carved Oak tree will testify to the power of names and symbols in love work, and hoodoo is no exception.

A petition paper is one of those things people fret over, but the basic principles are not difficult. For love work, we want the name of the loved one we wish to bring back. To gain power over this person and place ourselves "on top" of the situation, we write our own name over theirs. The name is often repeated multiple times to add emphasis. An odd number is usually used, with three, seven, and thirteen considered lucky or powerful.

A torn brown paper bag or parchment paper are nice, traditional choices to use for your name paper, but I also like to write on photos printed from a laser printer. Pencil or red ink are both fine, but a black Sharpie pen will get the job done. The key is to not get hung up on the details or to fret that every syllable must be perfect or disaster is bound to follow. Hoodoo shows a much earthier common sense than that.

Using paper and glue or digital tools, a photograph of the couple to be reconciled is cut in a heart shape, then put onto a white paper heart around which the petition "love me" is written repeatedly in Dove's Blood Ink without lifting the pen. On the back, the target's name is printed three times and "crossed" by the petitioner's signature, to unite them.

A WRITTEN PETITION TO LET ANGER EVAPORATE

Rootworker and Santera Miss Aida offers a nice petition paper method to soothe a target who is "pissed off at you." On brown paper from a lunch bag write your petition in pencil, using the full names of both yourself and your target: "[James Jones] will no longer be mad at [Clara Thomas]." Place the paper face up in an empty votive candle holder. "I put just a little Tranquility Oil — YES, oil! — on the paper. Then I fill the votive cup with water. You can either put it outside or at an open window to evaporate. When it evaporates, it goes to the target. My Godmother in Santeria taught me this. I've seen it done a few times and I have seen it work."

BLOOD HEART INK TO RETURN AN ABSENT LOVER

Ruth Cooke of Alcorn, Mississippi, told Puckett, "Prick your finger with a pin, take some of the blood and write your name and your sweetheart's name on a piece of paper. Draw a heart around the names and bury the paper under your doorstep. Your absent lover will return to you at once." The third finger of the left hand — the wedding ring finger — was specified by another informant as the correct finger to use in this spell.

DRAW THEM HOME WITH A SUGARED NAME PAPER

In this trick, the name of the target is written nine times on a piece of paper with black ink, according to a Hyatt informant in Algiers, Louisiana. Place the paper in a mixture of Holy Water, sugar, and Van Van Oil — "but don't put too much of that in, 'cause Van Van is something, if you don't sweeten it, it'll make trouble." After the paper has soaked, put the mixture around the house, and the smell will call your loved one home.

A SWATCH OF CLOTH TO BRING BACK A LOVER

Cut a one-inch piece from the target's shirt, and baptise it *in your own name*, an old-time worker in Waycross, Georgia told Hyatt. Then, on a small piece of paper, write your name and the name of your absent lover in red ink, as tiny as you can. Fold the names together and wrap the cloth around them. "Tote it anywhere about you — in your pocketbook, in your shoe. He'll soon return."

For more on petitions and name papers see:
"Paper In My Shoe" by Catherine Yronwode

BAPTISM OF DOLL BABY, CANDLE, OR OTHER STAND-IN

In addition to names and images, a variety of proxies are used in hoodoo to stand in for ourselves or an absent party. Figural candles, poppets, lodestones, coins, and even figs or pickles can play the role of lovers in a spell.

To make the connection, some workers employ a version of Catholic Church baptism. The standard rite concludes: "[John Doe], I baptise you in the name of the Father, and of the Son, and of the Holy Spirit." After each name in the Holy Trinity is spoken, Holy Water is poured over the child or, in our case, the spiritual representation we have chosen for our work.

I prefer the version taught by Yronwode, who explains, "When you create an effigy-doll to represent a person in a spell, you have to magically link it to the person whom it represents. Sewing a hair of the person into it, stuffing the person's name paper into its head, or glueing a photo of the person's face on the dollie's face are all valid methods of doing this. Then, once the doll is complete, it must be told who it is. I was taught how to do this years ago by a black guy named Luther in Oakland, California.

"He held the doll baby in his left hand on its back, drew a cross over it in the air with his right index and middle finger (like a Christian blessing gesture), and then held his open, slightly cupped right hand, palm down, in the air over it, but not touching it, as he said:

[John Doe] you are, [downward stroke of cross on name]
And [John Doe] to me [cross-stroke of cross on name]
You will always be. [hand pauses over dollie for next part]
You will think what i tell you to think,
Walk where i tell you to walk,
Talk when i tell you to talk,
Do what i tell you to,
Go where i send you,
And speak when you're spoken to.
In Jesus' name, Amen.

"After the first three spoken lines with the drawing of the cross, he improvised or rapped the rest of the baptism depending upon the circumstances." Connection achieved, we can now use the symbolic proxy in the work of our choice.

LOVING UP YOUR DOLL BABY TO TIE A MAN

Yronwode clearly distinguishes between a doll baby or poppet used in a hoodoo love-spell and the "voodoo dolls" seen in so many films. No pins needed for this one! She shares a spell from a young woman who wrapped her baptised doll baby in her soiled underpants, cooing softly and sweetly:

> *"[Johnny], honey, I'm gonna let you in my panties now. That's where you're gonna stay. I'm gonna cover up your eyes* [covering doll's head with the underwear] *so you can't look at no other woman. You just gonna stay in my panties, [Johnny], until I let you loose."*

"The underwear was tied in a knot around the doll and hidden where the man could not find it. At intervals she would take the doll out and kiss it, sweet-talk to it, and rub it on her breasts to love it up. Then she would re-wrap it in the underwear and put it away."

ANATOMICAL CANDLES TO BRING A LOVER HOME

"Male member" and "female member" candles were once carefully carved from larger wax pieces, making their use a difficult rarity. Today we have lovingly cast penises and vulvas available in red, blue, white, pink, and black. To recapture a loved one's attention, baptise a genital candle in his or her name and then lovingly caress it, anointing it with Lucky Clover Vulva Oil or Lucky Swastika Penis Oil. Finish it off with your own personal concerns and burn it on a photo of you and your target.

I prefer the Penis and Vulva Oils over hoodoo condition oils in this work. Formulated to be skin-friendly, the massage oils let you freely, and messily, embrace the job at hand.

When choosing a colour, think of how you want your lover to be when he or she comes back to you. Passionate, fiery, and sensual? Then go for red. If anger is an issue and you need peace and gentleness at home, blue is best. For romance and sweetness, try prink. When forgiveness, blessings, and a return to honouring one's marriage vows are desired, white candles work well.

For more on doll babies see:
"The Black Folder" edited by Catherine Yronwode

Tumba Walla, Bumba Walla, Return To Me

A well-known hoodoo doctor of New Orleans, Ruth Mason (named as "Kitty Brown" in *Mules and Men*) was a Catholic worker who took her student Zora Neale Hurston to a powerful "hoodoo dance" called to bring a death curse upon a man who had jilted his girlfriend. "Ruth began by teaching me various ways of bringing back a man or woman who had left his or her mate," Hurston wrote in "Hoodoo In America" — and the next eight spells are some of Mason's excellent love tricks.

SIX RED CANDLES, SIXTY PINS EACH

"Use six red candles. Stick sixty pins in each candle — thirty on each side. When you are sticking the pins in the candles, keep repeating: 'Tumba Walla, Bumba Walla, bring [Name] back to me.' Write the name of the person to be brought back three times on a small square of paper and stick it underneath the candle. Burn one of these prepared candles each night for six nights. Make six slips of paper and write the name of the wanderer once on each slip. Then put a pin in the paper on all four sides of the name. Each morning take the sixty pins left from the burning of the candle. Then smoke the slip of paper with the four pins in it in incense smoke and bury it with the pins under your door step. The piece of paper with the name written on it three times (upon which each candle stands while burning) must be kept each day until the last candle is burned. Then bury it in the same hole with the rest." This one tries my patience just thinking about it!

LEFT FOOT SOCK TO RETURN A MAN

Mason specified this one as a spell only to be used for working on a man. "Write his name three time. Dig a hole in the ground. Get a left-foot soiled sock from him secretly. His hatband may be used also. Put the paper with the name in the hole first. Then the sock or hatband. Then light a red candle on top of it all and burn it. Put a fresh sprig of Sweet Basil in a glass of water beside the candle. Light the candle at noon and burn until one. Light it again at 6:00 pm and burn it till 7:00. (Always pinch out a candle — never blow it out.) After the candle is lit, turn a barrel over the hole. When you get it in place, knock on it three times to call the spirit and say: 'Tumba Walla, Bumba Walla, bring [Name] home to me.'"

NINE RED CANDLES TO RETURN A SWEETHEART

Ruth Mason told Hurston to take nine deep red or pink candles and write the absent person's name on each candle, using a needle. Then write the name three times on paper. Put the paper in a cup, pour Van Van in the cup on the paper and dress all the candles with Van Van. Burn one of these candles every day at the hours of seven, nine, or eleven. Call the name of the party three times as each candle is burned.

QUICKSILVER TO BRING BACK AN ABSENT PARTY

I include this as a curiosity only! "Write the name of the absent party six times on paper. Put the paper in a water glass with two tablespoons full of quicksilver on it. Write his or her name three times each on six candles and burn one on a window sill in the daytime for six days." Quicksilver (Mercury), is poisonous, so use Return To Me Oil instead!

NINE LUMP LOAF SUGAR RETURN TO ME SPELL

To reconcile a marriage, Mason said, "Take the following mixture and sprinkle it over nine lumps of loaf sugar: essence of Van Van, essence of Geranium, essence of Lavender. Go nine blocks from the house and turn around and drop one lump of sugar in each block all the way back to the house, and he will make up with you." This spell works as a "trail of breadcrumbs," creating a path to draw someone to you.

TO CHANGE A MAN'S MIND ABOUT GOING AWAY

"Take his left shoe, set it up straight, then roll it one-half over first to the right, then to the left. Roll it to a coming-in door and point it straight in the door, and he can't leave. His hatband or sock can be made into a ball and rolled the same way; but it must be put under the sill or over the door." The shoe is used as both personal concern and proxy to bring the subject inside.

TWO NEW MOON SPELLS TO MAKE A MAN LOVE YOU

Wait until the new moon, and do either spell for nine days.

(1) Add a drop of your own urine each day to his tea or coffee, and you can lead him by the nose.

(2) Soak your foot in warm water, scrape it, put the water in his food, and you can be the boss. "Scrape from the toe to the heel — that's coming to you all the time," Mason said.

H.U. Lampe's Famous Spells

In 1974, *Famous Voodoo Rituals and Spells* by H. U. Lampe, a pseudonym of the candle shop owner Larry B. Wright, helped muddy the hoodoo-Voodoo waters. The book compiled both authentic hoodoo spells alongside the more saleable Voodoo name, divinities (lwas), and markings (veves). Lampe recorded an assortment of love spells — some from earlier sources without attribution, and many that featured commercial hoodoo preparations and unexpected magical references.

RED WITCH CANDLE LOVE SPELL
Anoint a red figural witch-shaped candle with Cleo May, Lovers, and Controlling Oils. Say, "Red Witch, let this offering to you bring my lover [Name] to me alone and for evermore." Burn for at least ten minutes, repeating on successive nights until love is secure. For a stronger effect, you may also burn Fire Of Love Incense, performing the ritual after sunset.

COME TO ME CANDLE AND INCENSE FOR RETURN
To bring back a lover, anoint a pink candle with Come To Me Oil. After sundown, light the candle and speak the loved one's name three times, asking for a return. Extinguish the candle after 15 minutes. Repeat nightly. On the sixth night, mix Come To Me Oil with Myrrh, Frankincense, or an incense such as Lovers or Commanding. Light the candle and say aloud, "Akmas Akmas Honah Haitunin Bisumin Honah Gedu." (These last words, oddly enough, are from an Iraqi love spell collected by R. Campbell Thompson, M.A. for "The Folk-lore of Mossoul," published in the *Proceedings of the Society of Biblical Archaeology* in 1906.)

STAY AT HOME POWDER SPELL
To use this powder to keep a wandering mate at home, sprinkle it on his or her clothes. If this does not prove adequate, a further ritual may be performed. Every night for seven nights, bathe before retiring and anoint the body with a small amount of Stay At Home Powder. On the eighth night, bathe and powder again. Write these words on a piece of paper — "SATOR AREPO TENET OPERA ROTAS" — and place it under your pillow. (The Sator Square is found all over, from Pompei in 79 A.D. to the famed 1820 Pennsylvania grimoire, George Hohman's *Long Lost Friend*.)

Star-Crossed Lovers

As with many a perfect turn of phrase, we owe this one to William Shakespeare, who opened *Romeo and Juliet* by giving away the ending:

Two households, both alike in dignity,
In fair Verona, where we lay our scene,
From ancient grudge break to new mutiny,
Where civil blood makes civil hands unclean.
From forth the fatal loins of these two foes
A pair of star-cross'd lovers take their life;
Whose misadventur'd piteous overthrows
Doth with their death bury their parents' strife.

Star-crossed refers to astrology, and it is to the planets that we turn when looking for solutions to this condition. How can we tell if two people are star-crossed lovers? First, the attraction is overwhelming. And second, it just doesn't work.

With star-crossed lovers, something is always going wrong. Both are married to other folks. Their families despise each other, or come from different ethnic, socio-economic or religious backgrounds. They meet on the maiden voyage of the Titanic. That sort of thing.

When we combine the astrological charts for star-crossed lovers, we are likely to see an abundance of squares, the ninety degree angles between planets that warn of tension, disagreements, and anger. They also create undeniable passion!

Unlike soulmates — who feel like they've always belonged together, or knew each other in a previous life — star-crossed lovers find themselves going in completely opposite directions. Their thoughts and feelings seem inexplicable to each other. An astrological relationship report is often the "instruction manual" necessary for sorting out and, yes, reconciling the awkward differences that drive such couples crazy.

Astrological remediation takes on these unique planetary problems, harmonizing them by means of astrological oils, candles, incense, powders and baths. Such products have a staple of hoodoo candle shops and mail order catalogues since the 1920s. Reconcile the warring lights and planets, and love has a chance to come to the fore.

Love Uncrossing

An ancestral curse, our own stars, a mess thrown by an ex-lover, the evil eye — there are a myriad of ways in which we can become crossed up in the love department. A whole book could be written on how to break jinxes and take of crossed conditions — and it has been (see below!), but here are a few love-uncrossing spells to get you started.

TO BREAK A LOVE JINX WITH A CANDLE

Khi Armand of ConjureInTheCity.com shares this: "To remove a jinx on an existing relationship, write a petition paper using the names of both parties crossed by the word 'UNJINXED.' Anoint the four corners and the center with either Jinx Killer or Reversing Oil (use the latter if a known third-party has placed the jinx). Butt a red and black jumbo double-action candle, and write 'All hexes, jinxes, and curses are removed from this relationship' with a pin on the black part of the candle backwards (in mirror-writing) from the wick end to the center. Write "Love and peace have been restored to this relationship" on the red part of the candle from the wick end to the center, writing normally. Starting at the center of the candle, stroke oil onto the candle, away from you on the black part with the wick facing away and then toward you on the red part with the wick facing you. Melt the candle bottom so it stands firmly in a holder and place it on a heatproof dish with Dill, Lemon Verbena, and Rue sprinkled around it.

For more uncrossing, jinx-breaking and curse-lifting spells, read:
"Deliverance!" by Khi Armand

TO PUT AN END TO QUARRELS IN THE KITCHEN

If you and your mate always seem to be fussing in the kitchen while meals are being prepared, it may be that the room itself has a jinx on it. A traditional remedy for this is to sprinkle dried Basil on the floor and sweep it out the back door, because "Evil cannot stay where Basil has been."

TO BREAK A JINX ON YOUR SEX-LIFE

If a jealous ex has put a jinx on your sex life so that you and your mate quarrel in the bedroom and can't settle down to have a good time, mop the floor or spritz the carpet with Chinese Wash, then place a pair of Balm of Gilead Buds in each corner of the room and another pair under the bed

Averting The Evil Eye

Because true love is something almost everyone desires, it is also prone to cursing by jealous friends and family — often completely by accident. The evil eye is a type of jinx thrown by the covetous gaze of another, one who wants something we have — and may secretly wish that we didn't.

A surprising number of my clients have aunts and cousins who, they absolutely know, are crossing them up. My own divinations invariably agree. But these problems are not always caused by roots being thrown. Sometimes it's just the fact that misery loves company.

Terrors of the Evil Eye Exposed! by Henri Gamache was sold in candle shops beginning in the 1940s, and the evil eye idea quickly took hold.

UNBROKEN EGG FOR CLEANING
Where I grew up in Texas, an unbroken raw egg is passed over the face of one touched by the evil eye. A cleansing ritual for many jinxes, the egg may be broken at the foot of a tree to release its bad energy.

THE HAMSA OR HAMESH HAND
The hamsa or Hand of Fatima (Arabic) also called the hamesh or Hand of Miriam (Hebrew) is an ancient amulet for protection against the evil eye. Blue glass discs in the shape of eyes are also used.

ASPAND SEEDS BURNED TO TAKE OFF THE EVIL EYE
A Zoroastrian prayer to the Five Archangels accompanies the burning of Aspand or Syrian Rue seeds. As an Afghan man told Yronwode, "It is used to remove the evil eye from the children, and it is good for anyone. My wife does it for me and for the children. I do it for her."

For more on the evil eye and ways to deal with it, see:
LuckyMojo.com/evileye.html
LuckyMojo.com/hamsahand.html
LuckyMojo.com/aspand.html

Hoodoo Bible Magic

From the sultry Song of Solomon to the Secrets of the Psalms, the Bible is the most important book on any conjure doctor's bookshelf. It is employed for wisdom, guidance, divination, and as a magical item in its own right. Here are some of the best Psalms to note for love work:

- **Psalms 17:** For safe travel abroad and to help bring a loved one home.
- **Psalms 23:** For prosperity, love, protection, wisdom, and guidance.
- **Psalms 32:** To gain respect, love, grace, and blessings from Heaven.
- **Psalms 33:** To protect, unite, and bless the members of a family.
- **Psalms 42:** Spiritual guidance, answers in dreams, love reconciliation.
- **Psalms 45:** Peace between husband and wife; to calm an angry spouse.
- **Psalms 46:** To help a struggling marriage; to soothe marital tensions.
- **Psalms 51:** To cleanse and remove sin, especially after acts of revenge.
- **Psalms 62:** For forgiveness of sins; to gain the blessing of the Lord.
- **Psalms 96:** To bless a family and bring happiness, peace, and joy.
- **Psalms 97:** Used with Psalms 96 to heal, bless, and cleanse a family.
- **Psalms 98:** To restore peace between hostile families; to bless a home.
- **Psalms 139:** To nurture and maintain love, especially within marriage.
- **Psalms 140:** For tranquility; to preserve and maintain relationships.

Of particular use in reconciliation are the Lord's Prayer (*"Forgive us our trespasses, as we forgive those who trespass against us"*), Psalms 51 (*"Purge me with Hyssop, and I shall be clean: wash me, and I shall be whiter than snow"*), and Psalms 32 (*"Blessed is he whose transgression is forgiven, whose sin is covered"*).

Chapter Four of the Song of Songs (or Song of Solomon) is used to draw forth an absent lover, with its many verses of pure sensuality:

Your channel is an orchard of pomegranates with all choicest fruits,
henna with nard, nard and saffron, calamus and cinnamon,
with all trees of frankincense, myrrh and aloes, with all chief spices —
a garden fountain, a well of living water, and flowing streams from Lebanon.
Awake, O north wind, and come, O south wind!
Blow upon my garden that its fragrance may be wafted abroad.
Let my beloved come to his garden, and eat its choicest fruits ...

SOLOMON'S CHAMPAGNE BOTTLE TO CHANGE MINDS

A Waycross, Georgia, worker told Hyatt, "Take a black bottle — a green-looking bottle that's got a navel, a deep hollow in the bottom. Now anything that you wish for this bottle to do, you fill this bottle full of water right freshly out of the well or the pump and hold it in your left hand. You then open your Bible to the first chapter of Song of Solomon. You carry it in your dwelling and you read that whole entire chapter down — first whole chapter. Close your Bible, then you walk outdoors and make a wish on the new moon — make a wish and take one swallow right over your left shoulder — throw just as far towards whomsoever you love or anything like that, that you can. Tell it, 'Now I want you to work fast.' Three days' time you'll see a change." The sensual nature of the passage makes this seem a natural love working, though it was also specified for enemies as well!

A RECONCILIATION BATH WITH THE 32ND PSALM

Yronwode says, "If the break-up between you and your lover was caused by something that you said or did — an argument, a moment of flirtation with someone else, a lapse in judgement of any kind — your best chance for reconciliation is to beg for forgiveness."

Her instructions include a simple bath made with Reconciliation Bath Crystals blessed with a copy of the 32nd Psalm, which reads, in part:

> *Blessed is he whose transgression is forgiven,*
> *whose sin is covered.*
> *Blessed is the man unto whom the Lord imputeth not iniquity,*
> *and in whose spirit there is no guile.*

Begin by hand-stirring 1/3 packet of bath crystals in a basin of warm water as you recite the 32nd Psalm. "Take the bowl to your shower or bath and pour the contents over yourself from the head or neck down (your choice, depending on your hairdo), and rinse with clean water as you pray Psalms 32 again," she says. Collect a small amount of the water before the bath drains. Pour it on the path leading up to your door (the path along which your loved one will return to you) as you recite Psalms 32 once more. Repeat for three days — a total of three baths and nine recitations of the Psalms.

PSALMS 45 AND 46 FOR PEACE BETWEEN MAN AND WIFE

In the 1600s, a German immigrant in Pennsylvania, Johannes Gottfried Seelig, translated the medieval Jewish tract, *Shimmush Tehillim (The Magical Uses of the Psalms)*, into German. It was later translated into English and republished as Godfrey Selig's *Secrets of the Psalms*. Here is a reconciliation formula from this famous book: "Whoever has a scolding wife, let him pronounce the 45th Psalm over pure Olive Oil, and anoint his body with it, when his wife, in the future will be more loveable and friendly. But if a man has innocently incurred the enmity of his wife, and desires a proper return of conjugal love and peace, let him pray the 46th Psalm over Olive Oil, and anoint his wife thoroughly with it, and, it is said, married love will again return."

PSALMS 23 AND 42 RETURN TO ME PHOTO SPELL

A Waycross, Georgia, worker told Hyatt to take two photographs, one of yourself and one of the person you wish to draw back to you. Write the 23rd Psalm on the back of one and the 42nd Psalm on the back of the other. Place them face to face under your pillow and sleep with them there. Your lost love will shortly return.

BOOK OF REVELATION RETURN TO ME PHOTO SPELL

A worker from Sumter, South Carolina, gave Hyatt a Bible spell to bring back a man: "Say he's going with you and says he's going to marry you and then he jumps up and goes up the road somewhere. Well, if you got his picture, he just as well had gone nowhere." Place his picture in Revelation, head to the floor. Every night, before you go to sleep, talk to his photo: "Joe, Joe, come home. Come home, Joe. I want to see you. Joe, come home and stay home and make your mind contented and stop running around." Talk to him until you fall asleep, the Bible under your pillow. After the ninth day he'll get uneasy, and soon he'll be home. Then place your own photo, head upright, facing his. "Read a chapter in that Bible every night from the time he's home. And then you talk to it just like you're talking to him — like I'm talking to you — for nine mornings, and when the nine mornings are over with, you will be lawfully married. I've seen that done several times."

To read many more spells of scriptural sorcery see:
"Hoodoo Bible Magic" by Miss Michaele and Prof. C. D. Porterfield

How to Make Him Think of You

Sometimes lovers don't break up, they just drift away. Long distances, overtime at work, college studies, military deployment, failure to have sex regularly: These are warning signs; get your lover's thoughts back on you!

HOYT'S COLOGNE BOTTLE FOR A VISION OF YOU
This is a spell that Catherine Yronwode learned when she was young.

"Take a full bottle of any size of Hoyt's Cologne. Remove the paper label from the bottle. It should be clear all the way around. In the old days, Hoyt's Cologne came with a cork, but now it has a plastic screw-cap. Find a small cork that fits the neck. Crafts stores and hardware stores have these, or you can hand-cut one down from a wine bottle cork.

"Next get a gold-eye needle and stick it through the cork, facing point-side outward, so the the eye of the needle is inside the bottle, when you put the cork in the bottle. Carefully clip off the point of the needle with side-cutting pliers, flush with the end of the cork. This spell is about making someone look only at you, so the eye on the needle is part of the symbolism, and that is why needle points are not used, but the EYE of the needle is inside the bottle.

"Get something of the person — anything of their body that can be tied with a thread. A hair is good. So is a fingernail or body fluid on cloth. A small button will do as well. Tie, wrap, or sew the item with red sewing thread, put the end of the thread through the needle, and tie it off, so it will hang inside the bottle when you cork it, soaking in the Hoyt's Cologne.

"Now get photos of yourself (digital print-out copies are fine) and tape them picture side inward all around the bottle. Depending on the size of the bottle and the size of your pictures, you can wrap one all the way around, or glue several together to make a collage of images to better fit the shape of the bottle. At the bottom of the bottle, place a picture of your face, or, for a return to sex, a picture of your genitals.

"Finally, wrap the entire bottle, pictures, cork, and all, in tin foil, shiny side inward. This seals everything in place.

"To work the bottle, all you have to do is lightly shake it and command your target to see only you, to think only of you, to look only for you — and no matter which way that person turns, he or she should only have eyes for you. If he once thought of you, he should again."

Forgive and Forget

The one who forgives never brings up the past to that person's face.
When you forgive, it's like it never happened.
True forgiveness is complete and total.

— Louis Zamperini, *Devil at My Heels*

The core of reconciliation work is forgiveness. This is what makes it both so powerful and so difficult. We do not easily forgive, particularly when a loved one has hurt us. But if we carry around a scorecard, we poison any hopes we might have for future happiness.

We may think of our hurt day in and day out. The sorrow and anger at betrayal can be that great. But if we are serious about healing, we must *never* speak of it. This is not about "sharing our feelings" — it is about *changing* them from within. And every time we bite our tongue and go for a walk, we change our truth, little by little. It can take a year or more to truly "let go."

One thing we all do when hurt is to become vigilant. "Once bitten, twice shy," as the saying goes. But if we are conjurers — and we all are conjurers, to one degree or another — we cannot afford the luxury of suspicion. In constantly looking for a wrong to be committed again, we call forth the very thing we most want to avoid!

In my practice, the most used (and most highly praised) work of reconciliation is the Forgive and Forget ritual. Right off the bat, I must tell folks that it's not about forgetting the other person, but about letting go of the wrongs committed. The work begins with the client writing a letter to God. It is simple and to the point, composed of two parts.

In the first section of the letter, each sentence takes the form of: "I forgive [name] for [action] and I will never think of it or mention it again." So, for example, I might write, "I forgive Sarah for lying about me to her mother and I will never think of it or mention it again."

One mistake occurs over and over in these letters (and I work on them with my clients until they're perfect). Instead of forgiving actions, people want to forgive *feelings*. "I forgive Sarah for breaking my heart." Well, your *reaction* to what Sarah did may be a broken heart, but that is *yours*, not something done to you. After all, someone else might have a completely different reaction to what Sarah did!

In the second section of the letter, we turn the tables. Each sentence takes the form of "I am truly sorry for [action] and will never do it again." Again, care must be taken to ask God's forgiveness and mercy for what we have done, so we write, "I am truly sorry for not paying more attention to Shelby," and not "I am truly sorry for making Shelby feel unloved." These letters are quite specific, personal and detailed. One I received was eight typewritten pages, single-spaced.

Once the letter is complete, I place it on my blessing altar with a run of three vigil candles fixed with Hyssop and 7-11 Holy Oil, over which I have recited the 51st Psalm. The client places the letter on his or her home altar or dresser, alongside a white candle and a glass of water — or sleeps with it under the pillow.

On the final Sunday morning of the ritual, rise before dawn. Take a Hyssop bath by the light of two white candles. If you purchase Hyssop tea bags, just steep them in boiling water and add the tea to your bath. If loose herbs are used, you may strain the tea or not, as you see fit. Recite Psalms 51 as you pour the tea into your bath. (Reading it by candlelight can be the hardest part!)

When you are cleansed and purified, step out between the two white candles. Allow yourself to drip dry or wrap yourself in a clean white towel. Save some of your bathwater — I find a quart container to be a nice amount. Take this to a crossroads and throw it toward the rising sun. Turn and leave your sins behind you.

Purge me with Hyssop, and I shall be clean; wash me, and I shall be whiter than snow.

Reconciliation Baths

Aura Laforest's tremendous book *Hoodoo Spiritual Baths: Cleansing Conjure With Washes And Waters* answers every question you might have on the topic of baths. These recipe of hers pack a powerful punch.

AURA'S RECONCILIATION BATH BOMB
"Bath Bombs are elaborate," she says, "but they really do the job!"
The recipe makes a three day supply, and Aura recommends you take the baths on a Friday, Saturday and Sunday. To make them you'll need:

- Heart-shaped mould (a cup will do if that's all you have)
- 2/3 cup Baking Soda
- 1/3 cup Citric Acid
- 3 tablespoons Pink Himalayan Salt
- 1/2 teaspoon Neroli Essential Oil (10% dilution in Jojoba Oil)
- 7 drops Spikenard Essential Oil
- 7 drops of Frankincense Essential Oil
- 3 drops of Bay Laurel Essential Oil
- Witch Hazel Extract in a spray bottle
- 6 Balm of Gilead Buds
- Althæa Leaf
- Wild Cherry Bark

Mix all the ingredients except for the last four together in a large bowl. "Get in there with your hands and work all the ingredients together along with your prayers," she says, noting, "I suggest gloves when you work since citric acid plus cuts on your hands equals unpleasant burning sensation.

"Once the mixture is even throughout, spray Witch Hazel and work it in with your hands until you have a consistency a wee bit drier than wet sand. It takes about a dozen spritzes. Start with less and add as required — better too dry and a bit crumbly than too wet and fizzing as it dries.

"Push the mixture into the mould about half-way. Embed a pair of Balm of Gilead Buds, a few Wild Cherry Bark chips and a bit of Althæa Leaf in the center. Cover and fill the rest of the way up with bath bomb mixture. Pack well. Turn out onto a flat surface and let harden undisturbed for 24 hours."

AURA'S RECONCILIATION TUB TRUFFLE

"Tub truffles are a bit more work to make than bath bombs, and they do require a thorough tub wash after using them," Laforest says, "but nothing leaves your skin as moisturized, and they are the best of bath time decadence." Sounds good to me! You need:

- 1 cup of Baking Soda
- 1/2 cup of Citric Acid
- 1/2 tsp of Return To Me Oil
- 1/4 tsp of Love Me Oil
- 1/2 tsp of Sweet Orange Essential Oil
- 3 drops of Star Anise Essential Oil
- 1 ounce of Cacao Butter
- 1/2 tsp of Sugar
- A few drops of berry-coloured cosmetic colouring
- Two bowls, a muffin tin, and plastic wrap

Melt the Cacao Butter in a double boiler or using the microwave. Meanwhile line the muffin tin with plastic wrap. Mix together the baking soda, citric acid, condition oils, essential oils, sugar — and your prayers!

"I suggest the Song of Solomon," Laforest says, "and also gloves!"

She finishes her instructions as follows:

"Add the liquid Cacao Butter to the mixture and again work everything together until it is even throughout, then split the result in two (eyeballing it is fine) and put each half in a separate bowl.

"To one of the bowls, add about five drops of the cosmetic colour. Work the colour through so that it is completely blended with the truffle mix.

"Fill a muffin tin cavity halfway with the berry-coloured truffle mix and then top it off with the uncoloured, white mix. Pack the mixture well and then turn it out carefully onto a flat surface and let it harden undisturbed for 24 hours."

BATHING WITH DIRECTIONALITY

To rid yourself of negativity, such as resentment toward a spouse who cheated but came home, wash downward, from head to toe. Let it go!

To bring in a desired result or circumstance, such as returning an absent lover to your bed or receiving a message from a lover who has stopped communicating, wash upward, from toe to head. Stand in good stead!

Love Letters Straight From Your Heart

So first, the bad news: No, an email is not a letter. No, a text is not a letter. A letter is a physical object. Because of that, we can use it as a personal concern, or to get something magical into the hands of our target. Touch and smell are important here — and pixels of light dancing on a computer screen, while magical in another way, just don't carry that physical connection. In the following three examples collected by Harry Hyatt, try to imagine how similar results might be achieved electronically. I'll wait.

A LETTER DRESSED WITH A JOCKEY CLUB SACHET

From a worker in Norfolk, Virginia: "Sit down and write a letter — write a letter just the same as the day you first started in to courting." Include the line from the 23rd Psalm, *"Yea, though I walk through the valley of the shadow of death, I will fear no evil."* After you do this, dress the letter with "a high-diluted perfume such as Jockey Club. But be sure that this perfume is used through a sachet powder" — that is, use Jockey Club scented sachet, not the liquid cologne. Send the letter to your target. On the third day, visit his neighbourhood and stroll by wearing the same perfume.

THEY THINK IT'S RED INK BUT IT'S YOUR BLOOD

From Madam Wiley of Memphis, Tennessee: "See, I take my forefinger and I write you a letter with my own blood. Sit down and dictate that whole letter in blood. See, they think it's red ink but it's your blood, and that draws you to me." A powerful use of a personal concern.

CRACKERJACK DRAWING POWDER ON A LETTER

"She had quit him," explains the Undercover Man of New Orleans, Louisiana to Hyatt. "He was writing her a letter, you see. I say, 'Put a little powder in there, and I guarantee you'll get a answer.' That love powder that you get at the Crackerjack Drug Store. They call it drawing powder. The next couple of days he got an answer. She sent for him, and I said, 'When you go to her, hug her and kiss her,' I say, 'and just drop a little of that powder on her.' When I left them there, they were together. If a person listens and do like I'm instructing them to do, why they'll have a success; but if you doubt it, there's not much success."

A DRESSED LETTER AND MOJO FOR RECONCILIATION

A beautiful spell taught by Yronwode and worked for nine mornings in the pre-dawn hours. Sound like a pain? Then let that loved one go! For this work, you'll need:

- Whole Queen Elizabeth Root (if you are female)
- Whole John the Conqueror Root (if you are male)
- Damiana
- Catnip
- Juniper Berries
- Rosebuds
- Balm of Gilead Buds
- 9 pink offertory candles
- Reconciliation Oil, Incense, Sachet, and Bath Crystals
- Pink flannel bag to make a mojo hand

Carve both of your names on the nine pink candles. Dress each candle with Reconciliation Oil before use. Burn the candles and incense for nine mornings before dawn. On the ninth morning, reserve a pinch of each of the herbs and the whole root for later use (described below). Light your incense and candle as you did the previous eight days. While they burn, make a tea from the rest of the herbs, strain it, then dissolve a packet of Reconciliation Bath Crystals in the liquid.

Bathe in this, rubbing only upward, and air dry yourself, setting aside a basin of bathwater. Prepare a paper to write to your lover by masturbating and getting some of your sexual fluids on the paper, then letting it dry.

Dress the root with your sexual fluids. Put the root and the herbs in the pink flannel bag and dress with Reconciliation Oil. Write the a letter on the prepared paper, sprinkle with Reconciliation Sachet, and triple seal it with a drop each of bathwater, Reconciliation Oil, and your personal concerns.

Keep the mojo bag on your person and use Reconciliation Oil as a scent. Take your leftover bathwater to a crossroads in the basin, throw it over your left shoulder toward the rising sun, walk away and don't look back.

Mail the letter at once, before you go home.

SEX MAGIC LOVE LETTER A LA P. B. RANDOLPH

For this love spell taught by Yronwode, the letter-dressing and use of Return To Me Oil, Sachet Powder, Incense, and Bath Crystals are based in hoodoo, but the use of sexual arousal is that of 19th century African-American sex magician Paschal Beverly Randolph.

In addition to the Return To Me products, you will also need a pen, paper, envelope, and a stamp, as well as a small basin and a figural candle (bride and groom, genitalia, or the like).

"Like most love spells, this one is best worked in the early morning before dawn, because it finishes at sunrise," notes Yronwode. "Those who take the moon's position into account may wish to perform it as the moon is waxing or growing in size, because it is a spell for increase. Some women may prefer to perform it on the first day of their menstrual cycle, regardless of the moon's position. Those who work by the days of the week may prefer to perform it on a Friday, as that is the day sacred to Venus, goddess of love. The choice is yours."

"Prepare a Return To Me bath. Dress the candle with Return To Me Oil, light it, and light the Return To Me Incense. Bathe with no other light than that from your candle, saving some of the bath-water containing your personal essence in the basin. Place the basin next to the candle.

"While still naked from the bath, and still with no other light than your candle, write the one you desire a sincere letter. Sprinkle the paper with Return To Me Sachet Powder, then draw your fingernails down the paper in wavy 'snake lines' to mark it. Shake the paper to let the powder fall away and set it aside. Repeat with the envelope.

"Next, formulate your specific desire," Yronwode teaches, "by which i mean get it very clear in your mind exactly what you want — for instance, that the person contacts you, falls in love with you, visits you, has sex with you, marries you, raises a family with you, and/or spends the rest of his or her life with you. Once you have formulated your specific desire, focus the entirety of your WILL upon achieving exactly the result you wish to accomplish."

"Then arouse yourself sexually by thinking of the person you want.

"At the moment of orgasm, silently voice your COMMAND that the person must come to you and fulfill the conditions you have willed.

"Immediately after, physically relax into a receptive posture and ACCEPT that as you asked, so shall it be done."

"After this moment of peaceful acceptance and reverie, touch each of the four corners of the letter with your sexual fluids. Place the letter in the envelope, touching each of the four corners of it with your sexual fluids as well. Seal the envelope with a streak of bathwater, dampening the stamp from the basin as well.

"At dawn, dress in fresh clothes. Carry the remaining bath water to a crossroads, throw it over your left shoulder toward the rising sun, and walk back home without looking back.

"Mail the letter at once," Yronwode writes. "If you can mail it on your way home from the crossroads, so much the better."

Paschal Beverly Randolph taught the three-part sequence of sexual arousal above, terming it "volantia," "decretism," and "posism." Volantia is Randolph's term for using volition or will to fully focus upon a desired result. Decretism is making a decree or command at the moment of orgasm. Posism is a relaxed posture of grateful acceptance after orgasm, knowing your work will bear fruit.

For more on Paschal Beverly Randolph and sex magic see:

LuckyMojo.com/tkpbrandolph.html
Southern-Spirits.com/randolph-on-hoodoo.html
LuckyMojo.com/sacredsex.html

DOVE'S BLOOD AND DRAGON BLOOD LOVE LETTER

Doctor Ira Vands of Florence, South Carolina, told Hyatt how to get back a lost lover, "In Dove's Blood Ink, write your name going this-away, and write hers backward. Fold that up and take the Dragon's Blood Resin and put it on the four corners of the world, which would be on the four corners of the letter. Rub it on and put it in the post office, if you know where she's been at for the last two years.

Doesn't matter if you don't know the street number, she'll get it. And when she gets that, she can't stay away to save her life."

MAILING A LETTER IN A HOLLOW TREE

If you and a friend knew each other when young, but drifted apart and became separated though time, you may write the person a letter "in the air." Keep it short and friendly, but ask the person to contact you if possible. Seal it and mail it in the hole in a hollow tree; the tree's leaves will bear the message on the wind. Try this three times only.

Alive With Magnetism!

Matched pairs of lodestones are found in many hoodoo love spells, and the reason is obvious: the pull between lodestones represents the pull between people. A good lodestone exerts an eerie force, and it should be treated the way it seems — as a living thing.

Here's how a 1945 King Novelty Company catalogue put it:

> *A Lodestone has been held in high regard by the Ancient Romans, Chinese, Mohamedans, and other people as a Powerful Amulet and GOOD LUCK Charm; probably because the Magnetic Influence of this Stone was supposed to ATTRACT Power, Favors, and Gifts. It is said that the Ancient Romans believed that Lodestone kept Husband and Wife faithful, and made their Love secure.*

Lodestones for love should be chosen according to gender and carefully paired. A male lodestone has a phallic pointedness, while a female lodestone is all curves. We want them about the same size, so that they fit nicely together. The matching process, as Yronwode describes it, is essential. The lodestones must be sprinkled with magnetic sand to help us view their north and south poles. Then they must be hold together along their different sides. We're seeking pairs "in which two edges join together well along their planar, convex, or concave surfaces *and* also have the proper positive-negative charges that allow them to 'draw' or attract along these selected surfaces."

Lodestones should be "fed" regularly while they're at work. A sprinkling of magnetic sand or anvil dust will do the trick. It's also a good idea to clean lodestones every once in a while, particularly if they sit out on your altar. Brush off the magnetic sand and wet them carefully, gently cleansing them. Hoyt's Cologne or whiskey are both good choices for this process. What isn't? Water. Don't put your lodestones in water unless you want them to rust.

Lodestones can be baptised just like doll babies. Two male or two female lodestones that draw nicely can be used for gay love spells, and any single lodestone that won't play well with others can be used alone to draw luck, money, or success! Store lodestones in a glass bowl, not something metal, so you don't inadvertently "drain" their energy.

"FEED THE HE, FEED THE SHE"

From Ruth Mason: "Get his sock. Take one silver dime, some hair from his head or his hatband. Lay the sock out on a table, bottom up. Write his name three times and put it on the sock. Place the dime on the name and the hair or hatband on the dime. Put a piece of 'he' lodestone on top of the hair and sprinkle it with steel dust. As you do this, say, 'Feed the he, feed the she.' That is what you call feeding the lodestone. Then fold the sock heel on the toe and roll it all up together tight. Pin the bundle by crossing two needles. Then wet it with whiskey and set it up over a door."

MAGNETIC LOVE PUPS

By far my favourite take on the lodestone motif are Magnetic Scotty Dogs. An ad from a 1946 Chicago Defender newspaper says it all:

Like powerful lodestones, these pups symbolize the magnetic strength of true love. High powered miniature Scotties are the latest sensation among lovers everywhere! HE wears one on his watch chain ... SHE wears hers on a charm bracelet; symbols of constant devotion. Mounted on powerful magnets, these colourful pups draw to one another irresistibly, AND SEEM TO ACT ALIVE! Supply limited, order today.

Magnetic Scotty dogs being trained as "riders" on a matched pair of Lodestones fed for love-drawing. They can be carried in a mojo or divided as described above. Art by Charles C. Dawson and Greywolf Townsend for King Novelty and Lucky Mojo Curio Co.

LODESTONE AND 7-KNOB CANDLE RECONCILIATION

Mix Reconciliation Sachet Powders and dried Hyssop herb. Sprinkle it on your altar in the shape of a heart. Take two paired lodestones of appropriate genders and baptise them in the names of your subjects. Underneath them, place the name and, if available, personal concerns for each subject. In the wide part of the heart, the top third, place the lodestones (with their name papers and personal concerns) so the sides that attract face each other. Over the course of seven days, you will be moving them toward each other, as if they are being irresistibly drawn together.

In the "point" or base of the heart, place two Balm of Gilead buds and a white seven knob candle. Dress the candle with Reconciliation Oil, stroking it toward your heart. If you have a small saucer of appropriate size, you may use it as a base, else leave it freestanding.

Before dawn or just after midnight, light the candle and call your lover back to you. Read aloud 1 Corinthians 13 (which includes the words, *"Love always protects, always trusts, always hopes, always perseveres. Love never fails."*)

Move the lodestones a little closer together, feeding a pinch of Magnetic Sand to each one. Burn the knob of the candle all the way, then pinch, don't blow, it out. Continue this process for six more days, one for each knob on your candle, until the lodestones touch. When the work is done, gently sweep the sachet powder, Hyssop, Balm of Gilead buds, leftover wax, and personal concerns into a clean white handkerchief, setting aside the lodestones for future work on these subjects. Tie the spell remnants with red string and bury it — near the front door if your loved one has left, in the backyard if you are together but fighting.

A more romantic version of this working can be done using Return To Me products, Catnip or Damiana instead of Hyssop, a red 7-knob candle, *Song of Songs 4*, and a red cloth or kerchief.

For more on lodestones in hoodoo see:
LuckyMojo.com/lodestone.html

MAKING THE MOST OF YOUR MAGNETIC SAND

The magnetic sand, anvil dust, or steel dust that you have used to feed lodestones can be re-used if you just brush it off the stones, wash them in whiskey, and start over. Magnetic sand is also a great addition to love mojos, but don't use it fresh; it has to have come off a lodestone.

Please, Saint Anthony, Look Around

To most Catholics, Saint Anthony of Padua is the patron saint of lost things and missing persons, petitioned for help in finding anything from car keys to lost love. Even those regarded as "lost souls" may be placed in his care. Why? At one time, Saint Anthony was asked to find a missing book. Success came, and ever after, Saint Anthony has been doing his thing. *An Angel by Brevet* by Helen Pitkin features a typical exchange, in which folk magic and the Catholic church are compared:

"'Why didn't you save your money and pray to Saint Antoine?' asked Angelique, wise in the lore of the canonized.

"'I owe him a candle right now,' Toussine said, 'but I ain't going to pay him. You have to stomp your foot at him, often — he's a mean saint.'

"Angelique was not shocked. 'I wanted to find my little diamond cross when I lost it, and I gave ten loaves to Saint Antoine's poor before I prayed. I never found my cross, do you believe it? When I wanted to dance the Carnival german I was too smart for him, and I promised him ten loaves for his poor if I was asked to dance. Of course, the invitation came, for he wanted those breads. Never pay Saint Antoine in advance.'"

As this passage mentions, Saint Anthony's Bread — an amount equal in weight to the weight of the person who has been lost — may be distributed to the poor in appreciation for wishes granted, particularly by or at churches dedicated to his name. The notion that some saints are "mean" or that they only help when a promised reward is held back until one's petition is granted, entered into hoodoo via widespread folk-Catholic beliefs of Southern and Mediterranean Europe.

A variety of rhymed prayers petition Saint Anthony. My favourite:

> *Something's lost and can't be found*
> *Please, Saint Anthony, look around!*

In South America, and especially in Peru, San Antonio is a real superman, wearing blue robes with a yellow lily and a red heart, while the more "standard" image in Europe and North America wears brown Franciscan robes and carries the Christ child and a white lily.

For more on Saint Anthony in hoodoo see:

LuckyMojo.com/saintanthony.html

Heart Lights and Love Lamps

A man's soul is the lamp of God, which searches the
chambers of one's innards. — Proverbs 20:27

"While most modern rootworkers prefer to use candles, the use of lamps is far older and more closely tied to magical practices of Africa," taught Dr. E. at the 2013 Hoodoo Heritage Festival in Forestville, California. "Candles are simply unpractical in tropical climates. They melt, warping their shape, and burn too quickly.

"The making of magical lamps filled with curios and powerful objects was found in most of the tribes of West Africa," Dr. E says. "With the slave trade, the magical use of loaded lamps came with the Congolese people to the Americas and became part of many African Diasporic Religions, as well as hoodoo."

The "eternal flame" has long been a symbol of the never-ending power of the deity, accompanying prayer and devotion in many cultures. But the "magic lamps" we're after here are used to return love and reconcile those who have become estranged.

The kerosene lamp is the most commonly used in traditional hoodoo, since it was the brightest available and thus used in home lighting in North America for many years. Pushing back the darkness is magic in itself, but to use a lamp for return or reconciliation work, we need to do something special. The glass reservoir of a standard lamp is the perfect place to put any kind of herbs, roots, minerals, papers, or curios — and a condition oil can be easily added to your lamp fuel. The reservoir itself can be crafted of glass tinted red, for love, or you may use a coloured lamp oil for the same effect.

NINE DAY OIL LAMP RITUAL OF RETURN

A Memphis woman who had once worked in Louisiana told Hyatt, "When someone is gone and you want them back, and you haven't got money to pay someone to bring them back, write their names nine times and burn it in the lamp for nine days and they'll return. If they're in town, like here in Memphis, and left you mad, you burn that lamp for nine days, and from three to nine days they return. If it's in Washington, D.C., from nine to twenty-one days, they return to you."

RUSTIC HOODOO OIL LAMPS

As taught by Dr. E., these little beauties, which burn vegetable oil rather than kerosene, are both easy and practical, with a size nice for any altar. He used a one pint or one quart glass Ball or Kerr canning jar with the standard two-part metal lid and rim, giving us these steps:

- **The Lid:** Remove the top of your canning jar. Separate the lid from the rim. Carefully cut the lid using a sturdy pair of kitchen shears or tin snips. (See diagram.) Be careful, as the lid is very sharp and can cut you. Smoke the jar with an appropriate incense and dress with oil.
- **The Curios:** Any fully-dried plant curios, mineral curios, charms or other items can be added to the jar. Lightly dress each item with an appropriate condition oil and pray over it as you add it to the jar. As long as they stay submerged, they will not burn, so don't worry about fire safety; the lid keeps the flame away from them.
- **The Oil:** Fill the jar with a vegetable oil associated with your magical goal. For love lights, Olive, Sunflower, or Safflower Oil are appropriate. Leave 1/2 inch of space between the oil and the lid. You do not want the two touching. Add a few drops condition oil to the jar. You may dye your oil with oil-based pigments.
- **The Wick:** Because vegetable oils are heavier than kerosene it is important to use a loose natural fiber wick. The best is a 100% cotton woven bandage from a drug store, tightly rolled along its length and loosely coiled in the oil.
- **The Light:** Submerge the wick in oil, and pull 1/4 inch through the slit in the metal lid. Place the lid on the top of the jar and screw the threaded rim in place. Pray over your lamp and light it. It may take a while for the oil to start wicking.
- **Daily:** Top off your lamp each day, or more frequently if needed. The wedge shape cut out of the lid allows you to easily pour more oil in or add curios and condition oils. The wick must be pulled up through the lid as it is consumed. I use a small pair of tongs to do this. Never let the oil get lower than 2 inches below the flame or the oil won't pull up the wick and the flame will self-extinguish. When your wick runs out, roll a new one and replace it in your lamp.

LOVE LAMP CURIOS

For your love lamp or heart light, try adding matched Lodestones, Lovage Root, John the Conqueror root (male), Queen Elizabeth root (female), Cubeb Berries, Ginger, Cinnamon sticks, a Raccoon bone, Adam and Eve roots, Balm of Gilead Buds, Blood Root, or Cowrie shells.

To add a touch of peacefulness, try Southern John Root, Angelica Root, Basil, Lavender, Hyssop, Rosemary, and Sandalwood chips.

Protective elements include Devil's Shoestring, Angelica Root, Bay Laurel Leaf, Dragon's Blood, and Rue.

Amuletic and talismanic charms such as evil eye beads, crosses, rings, coins, Siva linga stones, and heart-shaped stones may also be used, depending on your petition.

SUGARED LAMP BRINGS HIM CLOSER TO HOME

A female professional conjure worker known as Nahnee the "Boss of Algiers" told Hyatt that, "If you want to sweeten a man towards them, or something of the kind, take nine loaf sugars and orange water. And you take the name of the individual. And if it's a white person, you write it on white paper with red ink; a coloured person, brown paper with black ink. You write their name three times with your name on top of the name — you're the party that wants this person to be closer to you, so write your name on top of their name. You fold it and you pin it onto the wick of this lamp and your oil, and you keep that lamp burning day and night low, but it must be a tin lamp where it can't be detected what's in it."

SEW HIS NAME ON THE WICK TO DRAW HIM

Another Algiers, Louisiana, informant told Hyatt, "You can take a lamp and you can write a man's name nine times on there and get sugar, cinnamon and steel dust. Take your number eight black thread and then tie that name up with nine knots and sew it on the wick. When you sew it on the wick, you get a piece of red flannel and put in there, and that will draw him. Don't care where he is, you know, he gets worried and his mind will just roll across — it keeps him with a rolling headache and his mind just lives right on you. If he don't get to you, he'll soon go crazy in a few days. Keep that lamp continually burning. You buy a box of matches and you buy a nickel's oil, you see, and don't let no one light off it and don't you light off it yourself. Just keep it continually burning."

THE CLASSIC MOVING CANDLE SPELL

A moving candle spell for return and reconciliation is much like a spell performed with two Lodestones, only two candles are used instead.

Select two matching candles. They can be 9" jumbos, 6" offertories, 4" altar lights, 7-knobs, tapers, master candles, genital-shaped candles, naked human figural candles, pull-outs not in a glass, pillars, votives used as stubbies (that is, not in votive holders), or birthday candles.

As far as colours go, choose white for purity, pink for romantic reconciliation, red for sexual renewal, and blue for peace. Nine times out of ten, people choose red and are very happy with that selection.

If the candles cannot stand alone, you will need two holders.

You will need an oil to dress the candles. For this classic spell, choose a classic oil — Return To Me or Reconciliation — or both. If you like blending oils, add Love Me; it has a hint of sweetness.

Name one candle for yourself and one for your lover. Using a needle or a pen-knife write your name on your candle, either vertically or in a spiral going round like a barber-pole. Do the same on your lover's. If you have personal concerns, carve a little hole in the bottom of each candle and "load" it. Seal the load and fill the hole with melted wax.

Rub the oil or oil-blend onto the candles, from the bottom to the wicks, speaking of love as you do so. If they are figural candles, pay special attention to the intimate body-parts as you dress them. Set the candles in their holders if they are not the kind that stand alone.

On a fire-safe surface, set the candles at least 12" apart from one another, facing each other if they are figurals. Light yours first, then your lover's. As they burn, move them closer and closer together. You can do this all in one night or in sections over several nights.

If you want your lover to return to you, keep your candle in place and move your lover's toward yours. If you want to meet halfway, then move them each toward the other.

WORKING WITH FIGURAL CANDLES: TYING THE LOINS

If you selected Adam and Eve figural candles, you may conclude the spell by "tying the loins." Burn the candles for 15 minutes per day, pinch them out, and let them rest until the next day. As you move them closer each day, wrap sewing thread around their loins, tying them tight together. Let them burn out in place once they've been tied.

THREE-CANDLE LOVE SPELL FOR REUNION

This is a nine-day love spell taught by Yronwode that uses three candles — white, pink, and red — to successively attract someone, induce romantic feelings in them, and engender passionate reunion. Three figural couple candles (Bride and Groom or Adam and Eve) are needed, in white, pink, and red, plus a love oil — or several:

- **Love Me:** General purpose love drawing.
- **Return To Me:** To draw someone back to you.
- **Reconciliation:** To dissolve hurt and pain.
- **Follow Me Boy:** For female domination; to move a man to you.
- **Follow Me Girl:** For male domination; to move a woman to you.
- **Lavender Love Drops:** For gay or lesbian relationships.
- **Chuparrosa:** For honesty, sweetness, and gentleness.

You can use three different oils (one for each candle) or mix them.

Take a spiritual love bath before dawn on the first day. Begin the work as the sun comes up. Create a name paper with both your names in pencil. Carve your full names on the white candle, then dress it with your saliva, saying, "[Name of lover], love me as i love you. Desire me as i desire you. Come to me as i come to you. By my loving speech and tongue, be mine as i am yours." Anoint the candle with love oil and light both wicks as you say: "Spirit of Pure Love, i burn this candle in pure love's name that i may be loved by [name] as i myself love [him or her] and that [name] will burn for my love as i burn for [his or hers]. Let our thoughts be one. Amen." Pinch out the candle at about 1/3 of the way down.

On the 2nd day, again burn the white candle at dawn, and say the "Pure Love" candle-lighting prayer. Burn until it is about 2/3 gone.

On the 3rd day, again light it at dawn, say the "Pure Love" prayer, and let it burn until it goes out, even burning the name paper.

On the 4th day, start at noon. Create a name paper in black ink. Carve, baptise, and dress the pink candle. Place it against your bare body, saying, "[Name of lover], love me as i love you. Desire me as i desire you. Come to me as i come to you. By the link between my heart and yours, be mine as i am yours." Light both wicks of the candle as you say: "Spirit of Romantic Love, i burn this candle in romantic love's name that i may be loved by [name] as i myself love [him or her] and that [name] will burn for my love as i burn for [his or hers]. Let our hearts be one. Amen." Burn until 1/3 gone.

On the 5th day, again light it at noon, and say the "Romantic Love" candle-lighting prayer. Burn it until it is about 2/3 gone.

On the 6th day at noon, say the "Romantic Love" candle-lighting prayer and let it burn until it goes out, even burning the name paper.

On the 7th day, start at sundown. Make your name paper using red ink. Carve, baptise, and dress the red candle with oil. Then, if you are a woman, dress the candle with menstrual blood or sexual fluid; if a man, dress it with semen, saying, "[Name of lover], love me as i love you. Desire me as i desire you. Come to me as i come to you. By the nectar of my body, be mine as i am yours." Light both wicks of the candle as you say this prayer: "Spirit of Passionate Love, i burn this candle in passionate love's name that i may be loved by [name] as i myself love [him or her] and that [name] will burn for my love as i burn for [his or hers]. Let our bodies be one. Amen."

On the 8th day, again light it at sunset, and say the "Passionate Love" candle-lighting prayer. Burn it until it is about 2/3 gone.

On the 9th day, again light it at sunset, say the "Passionate Love" candle-lighting prayer, and let it burn until it goes out, even burning the name paper. As it burns, bathe in pure water to which you have added three drops of love oil. Pour the water over your head nine times as you say, "Spirit of Love, i have done this work for love and love only, that i may be loved by [name] as i myself love [him or her]. My love is mine! Amen!" Set aside a basin of the bath-water.

The next morning, sprinkle some of the bath water at your loved one's door step to mark it, then sprinkle as you walk to your door and mark it also. Wrap up any left-over candle wax in a red cloth. Secure it with red thread, tie it, and bury it in your back yard.

ROLLING CANDLES IN LOVE HERBS

To roll freestanding candles in herbs, just barely melt a layer of wax on a cookie sheet over a stove or in an oven. Don't let it get too hot. Sprinkle on finely crushed love herbs like Catnip, Dill, shredded Rose petals, Damiana, Violet, Spikenard, Elecampane, Patchouli, or Verbena, to which you have added a few drops of Love Me, Return To Me, or Reconciliation Oil. Remove the cookie-sheet from the heat and as the wax begins to harden, roll the candles in it to coat them. The result may look lumpy and "organic." Don't worry; that's normal.

Signs of Love

Many are the signs of love — and such omens are one of the things we look for in the first days following a love spell. A favourite song on the radio, a name repeatedly arising, accidentally spotting our lost love on the street — all qualify as signs that our work shows promise. Who hasn't said, "she loves me, she loves me not" while plucking a daisy?

YOUR FUTURE MATE

Twisting the stem of an apple while reciting the alphabet is a classic spell to discover the first initial of your future mate.

Puckett told an English charm shared by Frank Dickerson of Columbus, Mississippi: Place a green pea pod with nine peas in it over the kitchen door. The first person of the opposite sex who enters is your future mate.

Hattie Harris of Columbus, Mississippi told Puckett of "taking off her right shoe in the spring upon hearing the first dove of the year and finding a strand of the man's hair she was to marry."

R. B. Ware, of Atlanta, Georgia, related to Puckett that a girl, on seeing the new moon, should recite:

> New moon, pray tell me,
> Who my husband is to be;
> The colour of his hair,
> The clothes he is to wear,
> And the happy day he'll wed me.

The man she dreams of that night is to be her husband.

Dreams are a special form of connection with the beloved. When we want someone to return to us, we send ourselves into their dreams, making them think of us fondly. But this is where it's vital to inject a dose of reality, for if the person we desire does not know how to reach us, the astral effort is moot! "I have dreamed quite wonderfully of men i liked years ago in school, renewing our friendships, even becoming lovers in these dreams," writes Yronwode, "but i have no idea where they live now, or how to contact them. If they were working love spells on me, they left out an important factor: i got the 'message,' but i could not figure out a way to get in touch with them in return."

RED IS FOR LOVE AND A KEY FORETELLS LUCK

In 1891's *Gypsy Sorcery And Fortune Telling*, Charles Godfrey Leland told of a pleasing sign: "He or she who finds a red ribbon. tape, or even a piece of red stuff of any kind, especially if it be wool, will have luck in love. It must be picked up and carried as an amulet, and when raising it from the ground, the finder must make a wish for the love of some person. A yellow ribbon or flower, especially if floating on water, presages gold; a white object, silver, or peace or reconciliation."

It is also lucky for love to find a key, he said. Very old keys are valuable amulets for opening doors of the heart.

LOVE FLOATS TO THE TOP

An old-style root worker of Savannah, Georgia, told Hyatt, "You take the photograph when in love and put it in a basin of water, and if it floats on top, you and her will be in good love; but if it goes to the bottom, she wants to run away from you just as far as she can get."

READING THE WAX FOR SIGNS

Yronwode's long experience with love candles has given her an insight in reading signs in wax:

"If the bride side of a bride-and-groom candle — or a separate female candle — burns faster than the groom side — or a separate male candle — then she's more affected by the spell work than he is, and vice versa.

"If the woman's wax runs around the base of the man's, she's trying to cling to him, and vice versa."

WATCHING THE FLAME FOR OMENS

Candle flames are also of note, Yronwode says:

"If you are burning two or more candles, named for specific people, and the flame of one tends to lean or bend toward the other, the person so represented is attracted to the person signified by the other candle.

On the other hand, "If the flame on a candle that was named for an individual leans or bends away from a named candle representing a lover, or if they gutter down, then the person so signified is emotionally repulsed by the lover."

For more on candle divination see:

"The Art of Hoodoo Candle Magic" by Yronwode and Strabo

Tarot Cards in Love Readings

"Some tarot cards seem to have special meanings in love readings and consultations about love spells," notes Miss Bri of AIRR and BrianaSaussy.com. "Because tarot is the most commonly employed tool in diagnosing love cases, it is important to be familiar with cards that may be significant to love clients." The cards she describes here were designed by Arthur Edward Waite and illustrated by Pamela Colman Smith. Their deck remains the most popular occult tarot decks in the world.

The Lovers: This one says what it means and means what it says.

The Devil: In the imagery, you will notice that the Devil card has the same figures present in the Lovers card, but they are in Hell and chained to a rock under the Devil. This indicates serious problems. Qualities like delusional thinking, abuse, or addictions may be present. It can also represent an illicit love affair or a curse on the love life.

The Moon: This card often comes up to indicate that there is a problem with commitment. One partner is not ready to commit to the other because of appetite — sexual or otherwise — or due to necessity, such as a job, career, or financial concerns that require attention and commitment that

THE LOVERS.

would otherwise be going into the relationship. It can also indicate that one partner is suffering from a lack of freedom and movement. At its worst, it points to obsessiveness and lunacy.

The 2 of Cups: This is a card of contradictory meanings. It can indicate deep partnership between a man and woman, man and man, or woman and woman. (Note that despite the evident gender of the figures, this card may come up for those who are considering a same-sex union either openly or not openly.) On the other hand, it can also foretell that while things look good on the surface there is a possible deception underneath; the contemplated exchange of cups may not come to pass.

The 4 of Cups: This is another card about commitment and making choices. Here we have a character who is trying to choose — whether to be committed to one individual or to seek the freedom to play the field in pursuit of many. His gesture of denial to the proffered cup may indicate rejection of an offer of love.

The 6 of Cups: Here we see friendship, a psychic bond, and a desire to be remembered. There is also a level of youthful immaturity. The two may have been childhood sweethearts or see each other as brother and sister.

The 10 of Cups: A good, happy card! Coming together with faith and thankfulness, we have the possibility of family, married life, children (or more children), a joyful new start, and the purchase of a home.

The 4 of Wands: This shows a solid foundation and a celebration for lovers, sometimes against the odds; a bountiful harvest of happiness.

The 9 of Wands: Suspicion and doubt about one's partner or the relationship are indicated, as well as a decided lack of sound judgment or clear thinking. It often points to old wounds from past relationships.

The 9 of Pentacles: A woman of grace and power is presented with two choices: a snail at her feet, representing a lover who is slow to come closer or to commit, and a hooded hawk, representing an unknown lover from afar or in her future. Which will she choose?

The 10 of Pentacles: Patience will be rewarded with extended family bonds, home ownership, and comfort in old age.

The 2 of Swords: Choices need to be made; boundaries need to be established. The individual may have to make a choice without all the information needed. There may not be a "best" time to make a decision.

The 3 of Swords: This is a classic sign of sorrow in love.

The 4 of Swords: Relationship issues from the past are getting brought up in the present and making the future difficult to consider. Arguments and disagreements of the past need to stay there, and both partners should be encouraged to deal with immediate conflicts only.

The 9 of Swords: A card of sleeplessness, it can also literally indicate being left to sleep alone.

The 10 of Swords: Deep betrayal; often points to a partner's infidelity.

For more on divination with tarot cards see:
LuckyMojo.com/cartomancy.html
"The Pictorial Key to the Tarot" by Arthur Edward Waite

Personal Concerns to Aid the Lovelorn

Puckett called these "small bits of conjuration [in] popular use":

HAIR FROM YOUR LOVER'S HEAD

Get as many hairs from the girl's head as she is years old, and carry them in the upper left vest pocket (Hattie Harris, Columbus, Mississippi). Hair from your lover's head placed under the band of your hat (Southland Institute, Southland, Arkansas and Mary Allen Seminary, Crockett, Texas), worn in your purse (Gladys Minor, Thomasville, Georgia), or in the pocket nearest your heart (Cleo Jefferson, Fort Valley, Georgia), buried under your lover's door step (Fannie M. Miller, Fort Valley, Georgia), or nailed to a post (Beulah Miller, Fort Valley, Georgia), will make that person love you; but, inserted in a green tree, it will drive the owner crazy (Mary Allen Seminary, Crockett, Texas). To reunite a man and woman, get some hair from the head of each, take it to the woods, and find a young sapling that grows up in a fork. With your axe, split the tree a little at the fork, and put the hair into the split. When the wood grows back over the hairs, the two will be eternally united, said Robert Bryant, of New Orleans, Louisiana.

BATH WATER

"Charms are made for every occupation and desire in life — loving, hating, buying, selling, fishing, planting, traveling, hunting," wrote Mary Kingsley of her *Travels in West Africa*, published in 1897. "For example, a great love charm is made of the water in which the lover has washed, and this, mingled with the drink of the loved one, is held to soften the hardest heart." We still see bath-water used in hoodoo in America; there are even blues songs that mention it as a love-charm.

HAT BOW

The bow from your sweetheart's hat is effective in love affairs (Maude Jefferson, Fort Valley, Georgia), worn in your shoe (Maggie Jones, Fort Valley, Georgia and Mary Allen Seminary, Crockett, Texas), tied around your leg (Southland Institute, Southland, Arkansas), or in your stocking, though if you lose it he will beat you to death (Beulah Miller, Fort Valley, Georgia). Thrown into running water, that bow will do you good, though in stagnant water he will go crazy (Knox Academy, Selma, Alabama).

HAT BAND

You could write a note and slip it in the hat band of the desired person (Fort Walley High and Industrial School, Fort Walley, Georgia), or pick up that person's track and lay it over the door (Evelyn N. Thomas, Fort Valley, Georgia). You could put a letter from your lady love in a can and throw it into running water (Irene L. Griffin, Thomasville, Georgia),

FOOT TRACK DUST

"Pick up some dirt from her foot track, mix it with the dirt from your own, tie in a piece of red flannel, and wet with the juice from a red onion. Carry this in your left vest pocket, and she will surely be yours" (Hattie Harris, Columbus, Mississippi). Simpler still, take up the girl's tracks, put them in your sock, and bury it under your doorstep (Ada Bolling, Calhoun, Alabama); or wear a little of her hair in your shoe for a day or so and then take it and bury it in the same manner (Bernice Boldridge, Piney Woods, Mississippi), or simply bury six strands of your lover's hair beneath your door (Ella Mae Lashley, Pincy Woods, Mississippi).

Girls sometimes win an indisposed lover by putting his tracks under their bed, or send away an undesirable suitor by putting his tracks in an ant-bed, recounted Cleo Jefferson, of Fort Valley, Georgia

To bring your wife home, get some dried Devil's Shoe Strings, some dust from her right foot track, and a piece cut from the hollow of her right stocking. Mix these together and "plant" them near your house. "She will surely come home no matter who is tricking her away," saidFrank Dickerson of Columbus, Mississippi.

NAIL TRIMMINGS

You can win a person's affection by giving him wine in which your nail trimmings have been soaked (Daniel Bottler, of Atlanta, Georgia).

A GLANCE OF THE EYES

If a boy can have his eyes meet those of his girl and rub bluestone in his hands at the same time, she is his forever (Ada Bolling, Calhoun, Alabama).

KISS YOUR ELBOW

And finally, Vivian Mitchell of Thomasville, Georgia, joked that if a boy could kiss his own elbow, he could win a girl. Go ahead, try it!

When There Are No Personal Concerns

A practitioner by the name of SweetLady asked how to make a love-returning sugar jar with only a photograph, because she had no personal concerns, so Catherine Yronwode shared this spell with her:

"You may not be able to make a traditional sugar jar, but here is a really simple way to make a picture spell in a screw-top Mason jar.

"Punch a hole in the lid with a nail before you start. Keep the nail — you will need it later on. A headless finishing nail is best, and it should be no longer than the lid of the jar is wide, as you will see.

"Inside the jar you will position two photos of the person. Both sides are the same image, so use digital prints or photocopies. Cut out a circle of the target's face. The disc has to be small enough to fit in the mouth of the jar. Write the person's name and date of birth on the back of each copy of the photo. Glue them back-to-back with a loop of string between the two pieces of paper, the way kids make disc-shaped Christmas tree ornaments out of construction paper. The string is a loop, tied at the end. It is positioned on the back of one paper disc, which has been covered with glue, so that the loop of string sticks out at the top. The second disc of paper is then pressed onto the first and the disc is put under a book to dry nice and flat. What you end up with is a double-sided picture of the person on a hanging-loop.

"While the picture-disc is drying, collect images of yourself. Collage them together all over the outside of the jar, and the bottom of the jar and inside the lid of the jar, but if you cover over the hole you poked in the jar lid, you will need to poke through that again with your nail, to keep it open. And hang onto the nail; you will need it again.

"Once everything is glued and dried, take the little "ornament" disc and thread the loop through the hole in the jar-lid, from the underside to the outside. Wetting it with spit may may this easier. As soon as the loop is outside, run the nail through the loop, which will prevent it from falling back inside the jar. This is why a headless finishing nail it best — it lays down flatter than a nail with a head on it. You can add a pinch love-herbs, influence herbs, or sugar in the jar — but not too much. Breathe into the jar and seal it. Wrap the entire jar, including the lid and the fastening nail, in tin foil, shiny side inward. The jar is now ready for use. Shake it up and the disc will jump around inside the jar in such a way that the target will see only you."

Overcoming a Mother's Manipulation

A client who went by the name LM told us that her ex-boyfriend's mother had manipulated him into breaking up with her. First she made him feel unsure that he was "marriageable material." Then she worked him so hard that within one day he went from continuously telling LM that he loved her to deciding out of nowhere that LM was "really angry" at him and they should "just be friends." Catherine Yronwode gave LM suggestions on how to overcome this maternally induced break-up:

"This is a classic case of 'in-law trouble.' Here are a few magical actions, in descending order of evilness and increasing order of benevolence:

"1) Curse his evil mother. For instance, burn a D.U.M.E. candle on her or cross her or sprinkle her house with Goofer Dust.

"2) Send his mother away. Use Hot Foot Powder, Red Pepper, or something of that nature to get her out of his and your life.

"3) Break up the overly-symbiotic mother-son relationship. Burn a Break-Up candle on them or use Cast Off Evil Powder to separate them.

"4) Bend his mother to your will. Use Domination Incense and Essence of Bend-Over or Do As I Say Oil to fix her so that she can no longer try to control either of you and will do what you say.

"5) Protect him from his mother. Use John the Conqueror to strengthen his mastery and Angelica root to protect him. Add Crucible of Courage for his will power and Fiery Wall of Protection Oil to keep her away.

"6) Bring him back. Burn an Adam and Eve or Reconciliation candle on both of you and use a seven-day Lodestone spell (dressing the Lodestones with Magnetic Sand and Love Me oil) to get him to return.

"7) Create a loving, peaceful environment to win his mother's heart and encourage her to suggest that he come back. Burn a Peaceful Home candle on all three of you and use Peace Water to calm her and arouse his love.

"And, in a NON-magical vein, i suggest that you look into the possibility that he has a mild mental illness such as panic or anxiety attacks or even obsessive-compulsive disorder, because a grown man should not be so easily influenced by outside forces. One way to determine what underlies his erratic behaviour is to question him about his fears. Why does he think he is unmarriageable? Why does he say that you are angry? Are these ideas based in reality or are they arbitrary and not amenable to rational discourse? His mother may be a manipulator, but he may also simply be irrational."

Love Spells from the Drug Store

"On the counter of one drug store," Puckett said, "I saw a big can labeled LOVE POWDERS. The owner was suspicious and could not be prevailed upon to tell me what it contained, but I gathered that courtship, after all, was not purely a matter of pretty words and flowers. In fact, very often the unwilling object of the heart's desire may be won over by these 'good love powders' obtained from the drugstore or provided by the hoodoo-doctor." Professor A.J. Aven, Clinton, Mississippi; Bernice Boldridge, Piney Woods, Mississippi; and Miss Alice Johnson, McComb, Mississippi were witnesses.

Pitkin mentioned drug store love powders that were made into a cake, though its power wears off after ten years. She wrote of the root of Vinmoin, a local name for Vervain or Verbena, which had to be special-ordered from the drug store; rubbed on any part of a man's body, it wins his love. Puckett made an intriguing connection when he said of Pitkin, "She also tells me of her husband [Christian Schertz, a German immigrant], who owns a chain of drug stores in New Orleans, having daily requests for love powder, male (pink) and female (white), to be used to make such cakes."

In 1937, Hyatt interviewed an "Agent For Curios" in Jacksonville, Florida. She sold supplies from Keystone, Lucky Heart, Curio Products, and High Hat Cosmetics, all of Memphis, Tennessee, and told of their uses:

"Love Powder is something that people use on them to be well thought of and you carry it and most anybody will take to you and you can get favours of them, 'cause they will cater to you. See, some people, it look like everybody just thinks something of them.

"Dragon's Blood Controlling Powder — the great women get what they want. Look at Cleopatra, and how she used these great kings. She told them what she wanted. Look how this woman married here the other day — the white woman. [This interview was conducted when King Edward VIII abdicated to marry the socialite Wallis Simpson.]

"Never Part Oil — you put that oil behind the ears and underneath your arm because it is perfume. And just a little on the hair, that Never Part Oil. When it is used in the palm of the hand, then they always put the hand on that one that they never want to part from. They use that oil on them but they don't know it — they never know they use that oil or a little bit of that powder in their hands and they'll put their hands on the mouth — that's the hand and they got them right there."

Love supplies, 1920-2015: Art by Charles C. Dawson, R. C. Adams, P. Craig Russell, catherine yronwode, Nelson C. Hahne, Leslie Cabarga, Charlie Wylie, and Unknown Artist for Famous Products, Sovereign Products, R. C. Adams, and Lucky Mojo Curio Co.

According to distribution practices of the time, the "Agent For Curios" collected orders from her friends, purchased at a discount, and delivered the products at retail. She shared a product list from one of the companies she represented with Hyatt, who carefully read it word for word into his wax cylinder recording device. Among the hoodoo products of 1937 were these botanical and mineral curios, powders, oils, and perfumes:

- **Adam and Eve Paradise Root**: Wear these lucky tokens about your person to win or hold your wife, husband or sweetheart.
- **Egyptian Love Powder**: Use Cleopatra's powerful method. She held her man. She used Sweet Oil over him and won. You can too.
- **Oil of Charm**: Is there someone you want to take by storm? Anoint your body in secret with this wonderful charm oil.
- **Courting Powder**: Girls sprinkle this on your sofa, settee or porch swing before your sweetheart comes...it brings the tenant to life.
- **Get Together Powder**: Does the one you love hold back and say *No* when your heart yearns *Yes*? Then this is the powder for you.
- **Controlling Powder**: The powder that husbands with flirty, pretty wives use and home-body wives sprinkle on roving husbands.
- **Passion Oil**: Are you a wallflower? Do the girls avoid you though they think you are a funny character? Then this is the oil for you.
- **Lucky Month Perfume**: Your Lucky Month Perfume will make you sweeter and more sought after by the opposite sex. Alternate odours with that of your sweetheart for the best results. A courting marvel.
- **Spanish Luck Drops**: Get your share of love and good luck. Anoint your person with these drops or on the one you love. The Spanish people certainly know how to love...
- **Romance and Lucky Oil**: Wonderful oil for those tired of waiting for what they want. Sweethearts, have love and affection. Get hot quick.
- **Love Perfume and Live Lodestone**: Never before have elements of love and passion, luck and good fortune been available in such economical form. Carry a lodestone in your pocket on important days. Sprinkle your underwear with the love perfume for important dates.
- **Follow Me Boys or Follow Me Girls Powder**: This powder means just what it says. Girls, do you go to dances to just sit? Boys, do girls give you the cold shoulder when you crave love and kisses? Get wise and sprinkle this powder where it will do the most good.

The Life and Works of Marie Laveau

The Life and Works of Marie Laveau (reprinted as *Black and White Magic of Marie Laveau*) is a very useful spell-book of unknown authorship. It employs the drug store hoodoo products that came into vogue in the 1920s, so we know that Laveau, buried in 1881, had no part of it. In 1931, Hurston copied the text in the *Journal of American Folk-Lore* and said she had learned it from the rootworker Samuel Thompson. In 1935's *Mules and Men*, she attributed the same text to Luke Turner, "the nephew of Marie Laveau." Hurston probably bought the book in a drug store in New Orleans when she was there in 1928. Given the place, time, subject matter, and her husband's drug store trade, Helen Pitkin may have been the actual author.

THE LADY WHO LOST HER LOVER

O, my daughter, you come unto me and say: "Good mother, the man of my heart has left me; he does not come to my house and tell me of his love. He passes me by without a smile on his face. His eyes no longer sparkle with love when he speaks to me. O, good mother, I beg for your help, for all beauty and sunshine have gone from my life."

My poor downcast daughter, it is written that the sun shall again shine for you in gladness, and to accomplish this great desire you will take the Essence of Van Van two hin, and of the buds of the Garden of Gilead one hin, and you will make a four-cornered package of the buds, and upon this you will put of the Essence of Van Van. This you will put in the raiment of the one you love. And you shall make a small altar in your private room and put thereon a holy picture of Mary. And before this picture you shall burn the incense of the Temple of Solomon, called the Oriental Temple Incense, every day, praying that your charms will cause your loved one to think deeply of you and that you shall never be absent from his mind. And before this altar you will burn one pink candle every day for nine days, and under the candle you will put a piece of parchment paper on which you write the name of the one you love so that the wax will cover his name, so that no one can get his name but yourself. And when you shall seek your loved one you shall not upbraid him, neither shall you talk disapprovingly of him; but you shall smile on him and you shall be friendly and true to him. You will do all of these things, and you will be of good cheer and pure purpose so that the gods shall smile on your work.

THE MAN WHO LOST HIS SWEETHEART

Oh, dear mother, you see your son before you with tears in his eyes and a downcast look in his face, for I have lost my beautiful sweetheart whom I have loved for many a day and whom I cannot forget. She is always in my mind and I cannot sleep for the thoughts of her. I see no more her sweet smile when she receives me. I hear not her sweet voice when she speaks to me. I would gladly give half of my life for another moment of happiness with her such as there were before she left me. Oh, mother, I come to you for help.

My dear son, you will send to your sweetheart a box of sweets and in each one you will put one grain of Pink Love Powders, made of the petals of the Pink Rose of Damascus. And the night after that you will call upon her at her place of abode so that you may speak sweet words to her, and when you call upon her you will have upon your raiment the Essence of Attraction. This you will put upon you so that she will notice it and so that she will ask that you shall put some of the same upon her, so that the both shall come together in one blend and in one odour. And to accomplish this you must use your wits and your persuasion so that she will be willing that you shall put the Essence of Attraction upon her. And in your shoes when you are going to speak to her, or you are going to pass the place wherein she lives, you will put on the Powder of Attraction so that she will be willing to come out to you and speak to you and hearken to your words of passion.

If for any reason she will not see you, or you cannot see her, then you will write her a letter of sweet words with much promises of presents and many entertainments and in this letter you will sprinkle of the Essence of Attraction before you send it to her. This so that she will do as you ask and see you again. And at all times when you write to her, pass her house, or speak to her, you will have in your left-hand pocket a piece of the Wonder of the World Root [Ginseng]. This piece of root must be completely sewed up in a chamois skin bag and on this bag you will sprinkle of the extract of Jack of Clubs so that you will win her over and so that the spirits of evil influence will not cause her to change her mind.

And be sure when you get her back that you will treat her with kindness and you will be true to her so that her love for you shall grow stronger instead of slowly dying, and that she shall have thoughts of no one else but of you.

THE LADY WHOSE HUSBAND LEFT HOME

O, good mother, I come unto you in deep distress and tears have coursed my face in the dark hours of the night, for him who was flesh of my flesh, the blood of my heart and the companion of my soul, has left our home and gone from my side. Gone in the wilderness where my cries of distress will not reach him, where tender words will not be heard by him, where the sirens and bad women will have sway over him and make him forget me forever. Darkness closes in and about me and drags me down to the depths. O, good mother, I who cannot live without him am sorely pressed and only ask for death without your help.

O, my good daughter, do not lose hope and faith, for the stars say that there is a way to make your loved one's spirit commune with you and to have him come back to your side, there to remain and to comfort and protect you. In order to bring this about, you will into your own house bring a magnetic horse shoe, that which is red in the circle and bright on the ends, and you will get of the Gold Magnetic Sand and the Silver Magnetic Sand, of each one drachma. You will pour of each on the bright end of the magnetic horse shoe so that some will remain on it. This you will do to attract his love again, and so that his gold, his silver, his worldly goods shall remain with you.

You will burn a pink candle made of pure wax, nine of them, with his name under each one so that they will be for him only. And you will wear a pink and gold garter of Saint Matthew with the witch's charm made into it. This you will wear on your left leg and let no one but your loved one touch it. And if he does not come, you will write him a good letter, and on this letter you will sprinkle the Essence of Squint drops so that he will have eyes only for you, and so that he will not see the charms of other women, nor will he hearken unto them, nor love them.

If for reason known to you only, you wish that he shall become jealous of you and that jealousy will be to your advantage, it is written that a Novena made of nine green candles shall help you. Under each candle you will put your name and his name together, written on a piece of pure parchment paper. One each you will burn for nine nights. This will make the green-eyed monster of jealousy enter his mind and he will think of you both night and day, staying awake in the dark hours of the night to think of you. Herein fail not, for your happiness and love depend upon it.

THE MAN WHOSE WIFE LEFT HIM

Oh, good mother, look into your son's upturned face and bear with him until he has told you of his troubles and sorrow and poured his tale of misery at your feet. The woman of my heart has left my roof and my place of rest. She has gone from me with very few words and has left me broken-hearted, for I have her always in my mind and cannot sleep for her face is always before me. Tales have come to my ears that she has left me for another man whom she loves better than she loves me or that she simply left me because she does not love me any more as she used to do. I come to you that you may quiet my mind and make her think of me, and make her come back to me and love me in the same way that she did before.

My dear son, your heartbroken story has come to me and I hasten to answer your prayer that you may take your place again in the house of happiness. For love is at the bottom of all things and rules the world. So in order that you may win back the love of your wife and in order that she will come back to you, you will do the following things: In and around the house, wherein you dwelt in happiness with your wife, you will sprinkle of the gold magnetic sand one hin, and if you still live in the same house you will scrub the floor of your room on Saturday with the essence of Rosemary and with the essence of Verbena mixed together in equal portions, but if you have moved and want her to follow you to your new home, then you will scrub with the essence of Verbena and the essence of White Rose. Be sure to cover well the floor and front steps while scrubbing. And you will go to see her and upon your raiment you will put the extract of Hasno-Hanna [Jasmine] close to your body and you will speak to her with sweet words and many promises that she will believe and harken unto you. And if you cannot see her wherein she dwells, then you will write her a letter of love and forgiveness and in that letter you will put of the extract of Bend-Over so that she will read the words written therein and believe them. And in your house you will burn nine candles of pure wax, red in colour, so that the flames of love shall be rekindled and shall burn again.

And after you get her to come to you, you will then take the pink love powder and put it in her shoes, or on her raiment, or on her powder rag so that she will increase her love for you and remain with you to her last day.

Read more great old-time drug store spells in this book:
"Black and White Magic of Marie Laveau" by ... Anonymous

3-Ace-Queen-7 Return to Me

For this working, we first prepare four couples photos of ourselves and our loved one — half the size of our playing cards. Take the Seven, Queen, Ace, and Three of Hearts from your deck. For this spell I like a low vision deck, since the corner markings are bolder. Glue the prepared "valentine" photo on the top half of the card.

Begin with the photos upside-down as shown. Lay each one out in sequence, saying the name of your beloved. Then flip each card over, reciting "Re-Turn-To-Me." Now the photo is upright, and the card markings at lower left spell out L-O-V-E!

You can place a fixed candle to the right and left of the sequence or make a cross shape of cards around a central candle. Do this each time you think of your lover. Then restack the cards, put them away, and think of something else: a magazine, television show, or an errand you must run.

For more than 100 spells with regular playing cards, see
"A Deck of Spells" by Professor Charles Porterfield

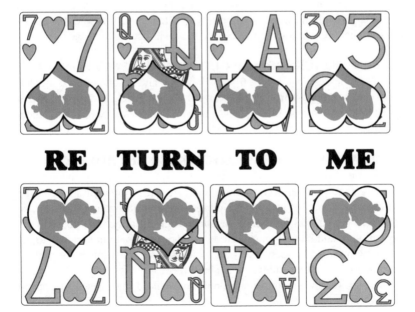

Miss Cat's Down-Home Short-and-Simples

Yronwode calls these spells "down-home short and simples" because they do not require the use of an elaborate altar or much time to prepare:

WHITE SAUCER, WHITE CANDLE, WHITE SUGAR

This is an emergency work, so start as soon as your lover leaves home. Write his name on paper nine times and cross it with your name written nine times. Place the paper in a white saucer and fill it with white sugar. Buy nine small white candles and burn one, set upright in the sugar, each day for nine days. If your lover has not returned after nine days, burn everything in a fire and do it again with new materials for nine more days. If your lover still is not back, again burn everything, and make a third attempt. If it does not work after three tries, your lover will not return.

ANTS WILL BRING YOUR LOVED ONE BACK

If your man has left town, go out at sunrise, stand in front of a Red Ants' nest, and call his name three times, each time asking the Ants to make him wander through the world until he is forced to return. It is said that all the ants in the world know each other, and they will get the message through.

FOOT TRACKS BRING YOUR SPOUSE SAFELY HOME

If your spouse leaves on a trip, walk behind and lift one of his or her left foot tracks, pulling it from the toe toward the heel, back toward you. Mix it with an equal volume of salt, sew it into a cloth packet, and wear it under your left armpit where you will sweat on it, until your mate returns.

WEAR PIECES OF HIS CLOTHES TO KEEP HIM FAITHFUL

If your lover will be away for while, and you want to prevent him finding another lover while on the road, steal the cloth lining out of the sweatband of his hat and wear it pinned either inside your underwear, so you will get vaginal fluid on it, or under your left armpit, so you will get sweat on it, and he will return safely. Another way to do this trick is to get the bow from his hat, sew it to your garter, and wear it while he is gone. If you don't wear garters, untie the hat bow, piece it out with a length of white string on which you have smeared his semen, and wear this as an improvised garter around your thigh while he is out of town.

Lover, Come Back to Me

Many are the means used to regain contact with an absent boyfriend, girlfriend, lover, or spouse, to bring a person to you, make them think of you kindly, or get them to answer your letters.

THE NINTH GLASS OF WATER BRINGS HER TO YOU

A New Orleans conjurer told Hyatt, "You take that woman's name and you write her name nine times with blue ink. For good always use blue ink, or indelible pencil, but for bad you use red or black." Red is often used for sex, but in this case, red could mean anger, so you use blue for peace or an indelible pencil to show that love won't fade away.

"You write her name nine times and you take and write your name into that, into hers. Get three little lumps of sugar, and you draw you nine glasses of water. The ninth glass you keep. You take that name and you put it in a saucer, in a plain white saucer — that's that woman's name and your name. You take that sugar and water and dissolve that good and sweet in there. You take that saucer and you put that saucer over that glass and you turn that glass upside down. You put that glass behind a bed or behind a door and get you two blue lights, and two white ones and two cream — that's six. You light all those candles at the same time. You put them there and I don't care if she's in New York, she's coming to where you are. You're gonna wonder how she got there, but she'll be there."

A HONEY-FILLED COCONUT BRINGS HIM BACK

A rootworker whom Hyatt interviewed in Algiers, Louisiana, shared a unique honey-jar spell made in a coconut instead of a glass container:

"Take a person's hair, toenails, the dust off their feet, a piece off the bottom of their sock. And you can get you a small Coconut — open that Coconut and take out all that water and put it to dry. Stuff all of that down in that Coconut, the hair, his clothes and the dust off his foot. Fill it half full of honey, and pulverize sugar and put it in there too, and you get you three Grains of Paradise seeds and you put them in there, and you have a little stopper and you stop that coconut up tight. Then three times a day you shake that Coconut, and I don't care if a man's from here to Italy, if you want him here, use that, and in nine days you'll either get a letter from him or you'll hear in some way from him."

A LETTER UNDER A CANDLE FORCES YOU TO WRITE

"If you wouldn't write me anymore, I could take — if you're a White person — I could take your handwriting and burn it under a white candle, demanding you write to me again constantly, and you would write me for the next nine days," says Hyatt's informant, the rootworker known as the Boy-Girl of New Orleans. "In some instances, if it's a Black person, you use a pink candle. And in some instances, with Black people, use a blue candle."

A HEN EGG UNDER THE STEPS BRINGS THEM HOME

"You're supposed to write a person's name on a hen egg nine times, if you want them to come to you," Hyatt was told by a Memphis Tennessee rootworker. "Bury that egg under your steps and at seven at night and seven in the morning, you call them. After nine mornings, they're supposed to come home to you."

RED FLANNEL AND PINS TO CONJURE HIM BACK

Robert Bryant, of New Orleans, La., told Puckett to get a strip of red flannel about a foot long and three inches wide, together with nine new needles. Name the flannel after the absent person. Fold it three times towards yourself, so that half of it is folded, saying with each fold, "Come (fold) on (fold) home (fold)" (or words to similar effect). Then turn the other end toward your self and make three more folds: "Papa (fold) wants (fold) you (fold)." Then stick the nine needles in the cloth in the shape of a cross, working each one towards your self and sticking each three times through the fabric, saying with each shove such phrases as: "Ma (stick) ry (stick) Smith (stick). Won't (stick) you (stick) come? (stick) etc." Afterwards get some Fast Luck and Jockey Club cologne from the drug store and sprinkle it on the flannel every morning for nine mornings, thinking earnestly of that person's return all the while. He won't be able to stay away.

RED FLANNEL AND URINE TO BRING HER BACK

Ed Murphy, of Columbus, Mississippi, told Puckett another, simpler method than Robert Bryant's: Urinate on a piece of red flannel and rub it thoroughly on your hands, then sit down immediately and write the absent one to come home. "She is bound to come," he says.

TO GET YOUR LETTER ANSWERED

A Saint Petersburg, Florida, worker shared a secret with Hyatt: "Well, there's different ways to make a person answer your letter. If you write a person a letter or anything of the kind, you take the names of three old women you know that died. Write their names down three times apiece — the dead people. Then take the name of whomsoever you're writing to, and write their name across the dead peoples' names nine times, and set it afire and burn it up, and they'll answer your letter regardless."

DUST YOUR WINDOWS WITH A BROOM

"Again, there is such a thing as someone having left you," said a Norfolk Virginia practitioner to Hyatt. "Go and dust your windows down with a brush or broom every morning for nine mornings and call their name. After that, sit down and write a letter and take this letter and burn it up. Throw the ashes in mid-air in the direction where you think they are. You will hear something from them. It may be a year, but you will receive some mail or message from this particular person."

A SWEET AND SOUR LETTER TRICK

A New Orleans, Louisiana, worker told Hyatt of tricks that can be done with your handwriting. "If you write a letter, they can take your handwriting and cause you to wander off." This involves drawing your handprint from the letter by dampening it with vinegar-water and laying it on a fresh sheet of paper.

"She's got that paper already sweetened with cinnamon and sugar on it. And she'll take that, your letter, and place it on top of that and sprinkle — just sprinkle where the writing is and draw that off of there. And that keeps your mind. To draw you, she'll just use the vinegar, but no sugar. If she uses sugar, it keeps your mind sweet; if she doesn't use sugar, just that sour vinegar, it keeps you angry."

A HAIR IN A CRACK TO KEEP COMING BACK

Robert Bryant, of New Orleans, Louisiana, told Puckett to get some hair from the mould of the woman's head [the anterior fontanelle] and some from her private parts. "When you are sleeping with her, slip out of bed and, unobserved, place the hair in a crack in the wall or floor near the bed. As long as it remains there your wife will never leave you."

FIVE TEN-PENNY NAILS WILL DO THE WORK

"Take five ten-penny nails — brand-new nails that have never been used. That's for him to come on back," said the woman Hyatt called his "First Informant in New Orleans": "If he's been gone for 100 years, if he's a-living, he's going to come back. You take them nails and you nail one in that corner, one in that corner, one in that corner — in all four corners of your home. And when you're driving the nails, you call the name — just call the name and drive them in every one of those corners.

"Go to the Crackerjack Drug Store and buy a red candle — a red candle, that's drawing, you see. Right now, if you put on a red dress and they had cows and bulls and things all out there, they'll run at you for that red. See, red draws attention. You write her or his name down on a piece of paper that's never been used, with an indelible pencil, and you set it right in a little saucer. Put the paper under the candle and you burn it for nine days. You light it at six in the morning and put it out at something to eleven.

"You take that fifth nail you have left over and that's the first thing he's got to walk over — he's got to walk over that nail. Now, when he comes home, you got him nailed down in the four corners of the house, he can't get away. If you say, 'Come on, let's go thisaway,' he's right there with you. I know about that candle proposition because my husband had left me, and a lady showed me how to do it. I did that and I know it works."

TO BRING AN ANGRY MAN HOME

Yronwode says if your man has left in anger, put a hair from his head, a hair from his armpit, and one of his public hairs in the toe of one of his socks, then roll the sock tightly toward you, calling aloud for him to return.

TO MAKE SOMEONE LOVE YOU AGAIN

Ruth Mason of New Orleans shared this trick with Hurston: "Take nine lumps of starch, nine of sugar, nine teaspoons of steel dust. Wet it all with Jockey Club cologne. Take nine pieces of ribbon, blue, red or yellow. Take a desert spoonful and put it on a piece of ribbon and tie it in a bag. As each fold is gathered together call his name. As you wrap it with yellow thread call his name till you finish. Make nine bags and place them under a rug, behind an armoire, under a step, or over a door. They will love you and give you everything they can get. Distance makes no difference. Your mind is talking to his mind and nothing beats that."

Graveyard Love

GRAVEYARD DIRT FROM ONE WHO LOVED YOU

A candle shop owner in Oakland, California, taught Yronwode a love spell that used dirt from the grave of someone who had loved her in life. He said, "Your grandmother, mother, father; your lover, husband, or wife who passed on before you — you get dirt from *their* grave only, and not from anywhere on the grave either, but from over the *heart*. Everybody has had at least *one* person to love them, even if it was just a little yellow spotted dog." The idea behind such spells, she says, is that "the dead one who loved you will work on the live one who does not love you yet, and will set their mind to thinking of you. That's why you want the dirt from over the heart of one who loved you — you want their spirit on your side, working on the mind of the one you love."

GRAVEYARD DIRT SPRINKLE FOR LOVE

"This is what they tell me," explained a Hyatt interviewee in Fayetteville, North Carolina. "You get the grave dust and you sprinkle it on the next person that you want to love. That will make them fall in love with you. If I want to make you love me, then I'd have to continue keeping it on you." Love forged in this way, even with the kindly help of friendly ancestors or dead lovers, requires continual maintenance.

GRAVEYARD DIRT, HOLY WATER, STEEL DUST, SUGAR

"If it's a good person passed out," an Algiers informant told Hyatt, "you takes that dirt and you get some of that Holy Water from the church, and you dissolve that together with steel dust in it — that's for drawing. And you take loaf sugar and brown sugar and a nickel's worth of gingersnaps, and you dissolve that. You want me now, you're drawing me to you. You're asking that good spirit — that's good graveyard dirt, you see — to do good for you with me. You put that around where I'm at, and every time I cross over that my thoughts go to you — that draws my mind right to you, see, every time I cross over it. But I come to you with a good mind, you see." The Ginger in the cookies is a "sweet-hot" way to speed up the work.

For more on graveyard dirt in hoodoo see:
LuckyMojo.com/graveyarddirt.html

Stay with Me

Now that we've restored your love, and all is right with the world, here are eight traditional workings to keep things solid from now on!

A MAGNOLIA LEAF IN THE MATTRESS
To keep a faithful marriage bed, southern women would sew magnolia leaves into the mattress. Nowadays, it's easier to tuck a magnolia leaf or two between the mattress and box springs.

A WEDDING RING IN THE SUGAR BOWL
We all want our spouses to stay sweet on us. When arguments arise, put your wedding ring in the sugar bowl to bring back smiles and kisses.

SOCKS OR UNDERWEAR BURIED IN THE BACKYARD
To keep your mate from straying, tie a knot in his or her bury their dirty socks or underwear and bury them in the backyard. You can also knot one of your socks or underpants to your partner's!

PUBIC HAIR IN THE HATBAND
Keep 'em crazy for you by putting one of your pubic hairs in their hatband, as close to their brain as you can get!

MENSTRUAL BLOOD IN THE COFFEE
If there were only one love spell, this would be it. Menstrual blood in coffee is the classic. Men can use a little chamber lye (urine) instead.

TIE HIS NECKTIE EVERY DAY
Tying his necktie for him will keep him thinking about you all day long. I suppose it can work just as well for women wearing power ties.

PRE-WEAR UNDERWEAR OR LINGERIE
Giving your partner some sexy underthings as a surprise gift? Make sure you wear them first, and the recipient will be yours forever.

STEP OVER A BROOM
Jumping the broom is an old marriage custom that's useful long after the honeymoon. Every time you move to a new home, step over a new broom as you first enter, then sweep out messes and guard against future tricks.

Frequently Asked Questions

The Lucky Mojo Forum, begun in 2008, averages sixty posts a day. It is organized into four sections: technical issues, Lucky Mojo spiritual supplies by form, personal conditions by type, and outreach to the hoodoo community (including contacts with readers, sign-ups for free readings on the LMC radio network, news about yearly workshops, and so forth).

Anyone can join the Forum and ask questions about hoodoo in general or about Lucky Mojo spiritual supplies in particular.

At the Forum, a dedicated crew of Moderators offers hands-on wisdom daily, dishing out spells, encouragement, and advice on the vicissitudes of life — fulfilling the role of the rootworker since hoodoo's earliest days. In addition to the "Mods," plenty of regular forum visitors also chime in with answers to questions, many of them presented from a background of personal or traditional family experience.

All of the Forum Moderators are graduates of Catherine Yronwode's course, and are compensated for their time in Lucky Mojo products. Some are also professional conjure doctors, and of those, several are members of the Association of Independent Readers and Rootworkers (AIRR).

"Spells for Ex-Lover Ex-Spouse to Return Reconcile Reunite" is a massive section of the board. As of this writing, it encompasses over 4,000 posts and is nearing a million and a half viewings.

The Frequently Asked Questions — and answers — that follow have been selected from the thousands of Forum posts about return and reconciliation spells. Here you will find answers to some of the most commonly asked and intriguing questions in the Forum

But first, some information about who is answering the questions in this section of the book:

Usernames followed by an (M) are people who are or were at one time Forum Moderators. Those whose names are marked (M, AIRR) are Moderators who are also professional members of AIRR:

Miss Aida	**Dr. Johannes**	**Miss Michaele**
ConjureMan Ali	**Lukianos**	**Devi Spring**
Miss Bri	**Ms. Melanie**	**Catherine Yronwode**

You can reach these AIRR members for readings, rootwork, magical coaching, or other professional spiritual services, at the AIRR web site:

ReadersAndRootworkers.org

• Is reconciliation harder than finding new love?

I noticed that many of the root workers recommended on this site do not do reconciliation spells. Is there a reason for that? Is reconciliation more difficult and complex to do than finding new love?
— mabel

Reconciliation work is, indeed, highly varied. (How long has the person been gone? Why did the person leave? Are there other people in the picture? Children? Etc.), and often comes bundled with lots of drama, conflicting emotions, and changing stories as new details come to light in the case. In addition, each day that passes diminishes the likelihood for a successful reconciliation, even with intensive spellwork by an experienced practitioner. If it's been more than a month (especially if the relationship is not of long standing), the prospects aren't good.

So, we have a combination of:

1) often complicated cases (and often with salient details omitted for one reason or another),

2) clients who may actually be more interested in revenge than in loving reconciliation, and who may actually sabotage the work being done, or, if the lost partner does come back in response to the spellwork, may drive the partner away again by picking fights, etc.,

3) a limited timeframe where work is likely to have a chance of success, which in turn leads to

4) a limited overall success rate for reconciliation work, in general.

All in all, a difficult type of work to make a career out of, unless one has an exceptionally high tolerance for both drama and failure, and a low need for providing effective and satisfactory services to one's clients. It is far, far easier to specialize in drawing new love for clients.

For these reasons (and more besides), relatively few rootworkers will do reconciliation work for hire, despite the high demand for it. That is not to say that there aren't plenty of folks out there who will happily take money from the love-lorn in return for "reconciliation work," but we are, for the purposes of this discussion, limiting ourselves to honest and ethical practitioners of rootwork.

— Lukianos (M, AIRR)

• How can I get my ex to contact me?

My boyfriend and I broke up in early January. I want him back in my life. Which candles work best to get him to contact me first?
— Renee

Get a Reconciliation mojo bag going, but also include some communication herbs like black Tobacco and Deer's Tongue Leaf. Dress it with Commanding Oil and keep the mojo in your pocket along with your cell phone. This is about establishing solid communication, so he or she may not call you within the hour, but keep dressing the mojo bag and keep in near your phone.
— ConjureMan Ali (M, AIRR)

A mix for quick and effective communication. Blend Deer's Tongue Leaf, Lemongrass, and Sage using a mortar and pestle. Make sure you crush Sage leaves so they blend better with the Lemon Grass and Deer's Tongue. Add a couple of drops of Mercury, Van Van, and Fast Luck Oils.
Pray over the blend stating your need/desire for clear, quick, and effective communication. Use to dress candles, in mojo hands, honey jars, bottle spells, or in spiritual baths.
— Miss Bri (M, AIRR)

Wrap a photo of your target around a parrot feather and place in a pink mojo bag. Insert some Deer's Tongue and Licorice Root and feed the mojo bag with Mercury Oil. The person will call you. If you do not have Mercury Oil, you can use Do As I say, Commanding, or Dominating Oil.
— starsinthesky7 (M)

Mix Calamus and Licorice Root together. Dress a candle (preferably a skull candle) with Commanding Oil. Drill some small holes and add the roots. Cover the holes with melted wax. Drill another hole in the mouth of the skull candle and add Deer's Tongue. Command him to call you.
You can dress a yellow candle with the same and command him to contact you. If you have Mercury oil, that would be even better as Mercury is about communication.
— Miss Aida (M, AIRR)

• Drifting apart?

My boyfriend and I broke up, and I got him back within three days by burning a red candle dressed with my menstrual blood. The trouble is, he has not wanted to have sex with me again. I feel like I only got him half-back. He is acting like a friend or brother. It has only been three days since he returned, but something is wrong and I need help fast or we are are going to drift apart for good.
— coastwitch

It sounds like you have him close enough now that a mojo bag would work. Get a hair of his and one of yours as well. Wrap them up in a paper on which you have written both his name and yours, criss-crossed. Fold two Balm of Gilead Buds for reunion, and a large pinch of Damiana herb for sex into the paper. Add two small Lodestone grits and Magnetic Sand for mutual attraction. Fold it toward you and sew it in a small packet of red flannel. Soak Damiana in whiskey. Use this to feed the mojo as you carry it on you. Sprinkle the Damiana extract at your doorstep and around your bed as well. Add it to alcoholic drinks if you can. Put your menstrual blood in food and drinks as well.
— cathrineyronwode (M, AIRR)

• Can hoodoo oils create something out of nothing?

Whenever I wear Kiss Me Now Oil, my intended says he loves the scent and he can't keep his hands off of me. When I'm not around he still contacts me but if I bring up anything romantic or sexual he seems to withdraw. Is the oil itself conjuring up these feelings or must he have some underlying feelings in order to be affected by the oil?
— ConjuringCat

Hoodoo does not work the same way as Harry Potter or Hollywood magic, but it can be easier to influence someone if they already have a hint or some underlying feelings of what you are trying to accomplish.

As a man myself i can attest to the fact that we have all kinds of things meandering around in our head and there could be a myriad of reasons that he feels the way he feels at any given time.
— ProphetAvery (M)

• What are differences between the love oils??

Is there a listing somewhere of the love oils and their purposes?
— LMFan

Come To Me is primarily to draw a new or unknown lover.
Love Me is to deepen a relationship, to move from platonic to romantic.
Kiss Me Now is for instant passion
Fire of Love is for sexuality, especially rekindling the flame.
Return To Me is to bring a straying lover or friend back.
Reconciliation is to heal a rift between lovers or good friends.
Bewitching is for seduction.
Marriage is for a proposal or to bring about a wedding.
Stay With Me is to prevent a separation of divorce.
Stay At Home is to keep a lover from going out on the town.
Dixie Love is for a happy marriage, faithful love, and strong values.
Look Me Over is to draw attention; it can draw flirtations.
Chuparrosa is for honesty and trust in love.
Peaceful Home is not so much a love oil as a family harmony oil.
Queen Elizabeth Root in Oil is for female, queenly power.
John the Conqueror Root in Oil is for male, kingly power.
— catherineyronwode (M, AIRR)

• What kinds of oils can I or can't I wear on my body?

I've read that some oils aren't suitable to be applied on oneself, except those for attracting stuff and people. Is that the correct way?
— JieXuan

We use all sorts of condition oils on the body, including Peaceful Home, Influence, Essence of Bend-Over, Jinx Killer, King Solomon Wisdom, Tranquility, Crown of Success, Do As I Say, Commanding, John the Conqueror, Uncrossing, Law Keep Away, Stop Gossip, Healing and Victory, none of which are for "attracting stuff and people." We want folks to touch, smell, and get all wrapped up in our oils, and if that includes wearing them, so be it! We do not, however, wear cursing oils on the body.
— catherineyronwode (M, AIRR)

• What are the love-controlling oils and how do I use them?

If the target loves me but due to circumstances finds himself helpless, then would Essence of Bend-Over Oil force him to talk despite circumstances or would Commanding Oil bring about that effect?
— path2success

What you are asking about, I think, is how to blend controlling-type oils with love oils, in order to take command of a situation. Here are a few of the dominating oils — but remember, you will mix them with love oils to use in any situation where your primary goal is unity or reunion.

Do As I Say implies that the target is someone you have verbal interaction with — it augments the power of your voice, and might well be used by someone in a position of authority to bolster that authority (or to gain the upper hand if you are not in authority).

Essence of Bend-Over is used by those who are in a subservient position to gain favours and favour from those with authority over them.

With Influence, there is an element of persuasion of the target that the commands of the worker are also the commands of the target's free will — subtle, not dramatic, good for bolstering persuasive powers over those with greater power/authority.

Commanding Oil subjugates the will (but not necessarily the initiative) of the target to the will of the worker — the target is like a soldier, following orders from the worker, who acts as his or her commanding officer.

Compelling Oil causes the target to follow the commands of the user, but those commands will not necessarily be perceived as "commands," per se — rather, the target will feel "compelled" to do whatever it is that the worker has commanded. Compelling is often used to encourage repayment of debts, or for follow-through on promises.

With Controlling Oil, the will and initiative of the target are placed under the control of the worker — like a puppet on a string.

Domination Oil is for unquestioned rulership.

I Dominate My Man / I Dominate My Woman are fairly cruel and harsh and are directed toward a lover.

I Can You Can't is a way to win against a competitor.
— Lukianos (M, AIRR)

• Do I need to empower my oils before I use them?

Is there a traditional way of charging up oils in conjure before use?
— leonus23

The herbs and roots are powerful in and of themselves, but it's the prayers of the practitioner that turns them into a magically potent item.

The Lucky Mojo oils are prayed over as they are made — so if you are ordering the Lucky Mojo oils, you don't have to take that initial step. That being said, you still have to empower your overall work through intent and prayer — whether that be dressing a candle with the oils, or whathaveyou. That way you tune the oils to work exactly the way YOU want them to.

For instance, the Love Me Oil is made with herbs and roots that work to attract someone to the target. Most often this is used in a romantic or sexual way. However, I always use Love Me Oil on items that I'm trying to sell — so when I'm doing the work of dressing the item with the Love Me Oil, I'm making the intent that it attracts people to love the ITEM. You're still working with getting a positive emotional reaction, but the intent changes that from romantic to something more general.
— Devi Spring (M, AIRR)

Our recipes for all of our religious oils — including not only Catholic saints, but also Hindu deities, and Jewish prophets — draw on traditional ideas about the spiritual being who is being called upon, and include, insofar as possible, a selection of herbs, roots, and minerals associated with the entity in the religious and magical folklore of the nation in which veneration of that saint, deity, or spirit first developed, plus any other herbs, roots, and minerals that may later have come to be associated with that being. For instance, King Solomon Wisdom Oil, in addition to herbs and essential oils mentioned in the portions of the Bible relating to King Solomon, also contains Solomon Seal Root, an American herb associated with King Solomon in American folklore and folk magic.
— catherineyronwode (M, AIRR)

For more on using oils in hoodoo see:
LuckyMojo.com/oils.html

• How do I use sachet powders to make him return to loving me?

How would i lay the powders down? Would i have to secretly do it while i'm at his house? As long as he steps in the powders will it work?
— vinavin21

You can deploy sachet powders either in places where your lover will walk over them (his place, your place if he comes over, on the ground outside his car, etc.), or as a dressing for paper or other items that he will handle — a letter, a pen, his shoes, etc. If you have access to his personal grooming items, you can add condition powders to them, especially if he uses conventional antiperspirant or medicated powders. You can also make use of any footprints that he leaves (in soil, sand, or snow), either sprinkling powders directly into his foot-track, or collecting his foot-track (toe to heel to bring him toward you) for use as a personal concern — one option would be to mix the foot track with condition powders and keep them in a bottle or other suitable container for further works. In all cases, you will say his name and state your intention as you deploy the powders. Also, be careful to blend the powder(s) well with local dirt, or the pigment of the condition powder may reveal your trick.
— Lukianos (M, AIRR)

You could also sprinkle the sachet powder (lightly) on his pillow, on his side of the bed, you could put pinches of it in his pants pocket, you could even dress his cash and coins, or anything he touches or fiddles with a lot with the powder to ensure he gets it on him.
— Miss Bri (M, AIRR)

I've also deployed sachet powder on chairs and car seats. Especially if he worships his vehicle, use the back and head rest. Some men seem to have a favourite chair or sofa to rest (fall asleep) on in the house. I powdered that baby down. Not where it's obvious, but he was sleeping in enough to do some good. I've also put some in a man's shoe as well.
— DNA

For more on using sachet powers in hoodoo see:
LuckyMojo.com/powders.html

• How and which personal concerns should I use?

I am thinking about making something for when he comes over. What should I add in the food? The drink? Is blood from a finger prick as effective as menstrual blood? Should I put vaginal fluids on raw cookie dough then bake, or bake the cookies first, then put vaginal fluids on it?
— PreciousCC

Take a bath in love herbs, save some of your bath water and add it to the food or drinks. Use Catnip as a garnish in the food, also Roses, Rose Water, Cardamon Seeds, Cinnamon, Ginger — the list is endless.
— j82

I would put the fluids in before you bake the cookies.
— Ms Melanie (M, AIRR)

The point of using menstrual blood in particular, rather than finger-prick blood, is that it comes from your lady parts, which is why it's used in love work. Sexual fluids are the most common alternative. After that, urine. And remember, you only need a few drops.
— MissMichaele (M, AIRR)

• Can I tie his underwear to get him to move back home?

My boyfriend moved out and I want him to move back home with me. I have a used pair of his underwear and was wondering if I can use them in getting him back. In Cat's book "Hoodoo Herb and Root Magic," it says to tie it and then bury it. Would that work even if he's no longer at home? If not, what other spell using his underwear can I do to get him get him to move back with me?
— jewel

Tying and burying underwear usually is intended to keep someone home, not to bring someone back. However, you do have a great personal concern in that underwear, so why not use it to make a doll baby and work with it as a proxy-doll in spells of return and reconciliation?
— NotDorianGray

• Can I dress myself or someone else "down there"?

My family roots are from the deep south, and growing up i heard all kinds of stories about spells. Have you heard of this love spell called dressing a man? Meaning before you have sex with him, there is something you can rub on his XXXXXX and after he has sex with you, he will care for you very much, and do anything for you.
— egyptianqueen

That and things along that line are pretty common. One that I've heard more often is a woman dressing herself down there so the man will drag himself through it. I would caution anyone that wants to dress any orifice this way to use a small amount, very small.
— Turnsteel

Honey, people all over Mississippi, Alabama, Arkansas, Tennessee, Michigan, California, and points east, south, north, and west know about this, and here at the Lucky Mojo Curio Co., we actually make the stuff that people use to dress their XXXXXX. :-)
— catherineyronwode (M, AIRR)

• Does texting count as communication?

Do I need reconciliation if we have remained in contact by texting?
— MunecaDePana

Texting is not good enough for staying in communication. The emotional component of your voice is missing in the text and he can't hear how much you love him in your voice. I'd recommend using phone calls instead of texts. You can also powder gifts with Reconciliation Powder and send or give them to him so he is hit on a physical level with your magic.
— Dr. E. (M, AIRR)

Reconciliation means to get back in alignment again. We usually use it if there has been an argument, but since people can certainly argue by text, sending texts is not a not proof that you don't need reconciliation.
— catherineyronwode (M, AIRR)

• How would I use his semen? What should I pray?

I am trying to win my son's father back to me. How would I use his semen? What prayers or Psalms will serve my needs? Also he has dabbled orally in my menstrual blood, how binding is that?
— faitlaforce

To use his semen, dab it in a five-spot pattern, like on dice, on the petition paper on which you have written your command, Then dab your own juices over it in the same pattern.

Roll his socks to you to cause him to come back, roll from toe to top, always toward you. You can also knot one of his socks to one of yours and hide it between the box springs and mattress on your bed.

Load a pink male member candle from below by digging out a little hole, and place some of his semen in that, too. That marks the candle for him. Then carve his name in the wax with a needle. Dress the candle with Follow Me Boy and Return To Me Oils. Place his name on paper beneath the candle.

For scripture, I would try Chapter Four of the Song of Songs, also known as the Song of Solomon. It is long, but powerful.

To answer your last question, well, they say that if a man gets a taste of that, he will always come back for more!
— catherineyronwode (M, AIRR)

• I can't get photos. Can I draw instead?

My printer is out of toner and I can't get a new one for a while. I'm a pretty decent artist, could I draw the faces of my targets instead? Does it have to be an amazing likeness? Or can I just use their names and personal effects (hair) without an image?
— ravenmaven

Absolutely draw their faces with your own hand, mind, heart and spirit! It doesn't have to be photorealistic — it's the act of drawing with focused intent that makes it work. And their personal concerns? Dynamite! All my best work has been done with real, 3D personal concerns.
— MissMichaele (M, AIRR)

• **How can I do love work that is less lust and more trust?**

I notice a lot of the love type oils focus on lust and sexuality. Is there something that can be used that helps one's partner to trust more and increase chemistry in a more innocent way?
— Brea

Do you think Chuparrosa Oil and products would work on sweetening a relationship in an innocent way, also bringing more trust into the relationship?
— Chaitanya

Come To Me, Love Me, Adam And Eve, and Stay With Me Oils are not just about sex. They cover all the bases. I like Sumac, Cloves, and King Solomon's Wisdom Root and Oil for love based on friendship. The healing- and peace-related oils mixed with love oils can do this.
— Literarylioness (M)

The Chuparrosa (hummingbird spirit of love) is most often called on for aid in finding a sincere and true lover, usually for a long-term relationship. That said, Chuparrosa can also be called on for help in sweetening one's life and love, and removing bitterness and sadness from one's heart.

The herb Deer's Tongue is well known as a useful aid in both promoting eloquence of speech and loosening tongues generally — good for promoting open communication.

Balm of Gilead is a healer of bruised hearts and may be of assistance in cases where a partner's difficulty with trust stems from previous hurts.

Condition formulas that may be of interest in such cases would include Blessing, Healing, Clarity, and Tranquility, especially if mixed in with an appropriate love formula.
— Lukianos (M, AIRR)

I work with a lot of folks whose loved ones are pretty damaged. Saint Dymphna is my go-to healer in such situations. I dress her candles with Clarity and Van Van Oils. A blend of Crucible of Courage and King Solomon Wisdom Oils is great for gaining marriage proposals!
— Deacon Millett (M, AIRR)

• **How can I warm someone back up to me?**

We got back together recently but he's telling me he doesn't know if he loves me or not. I am looking to get back to where we were. I basically need to ignite the man's passions and get his heart pumping for me again.
— XBlodeuweddX

Get Fire of Love, Follow Me Boy, Love Me, or Stay With Me. To reignite passion, work with the first two; to keep him bound to you, use the last two. Dust your clothing, toss a bit of the bath crystals in the wash with his clothes, wear the oils as a scent. Make a honey or sugar jar to keep him sweet to you. Anoint a red candle with your sexual fluids and burn it on a picture of his, or on a petition paper for him to love you. Add one of the oils in conjunction with the fluids.
— ConjureMan Ali (M, AIRR)

• **What reuniting work can I do when he's physically present?**

What can I do to rekindle love whilst I am in his physical presence?
— moonchild

Give him a letter, a check, cash, or a card, dusted with Return To Me sachet powders. If you are on your period, sneak him some of your menstrual blood. Wear love-drawing condition oils as your "perfume."
— Miss Bri (M, AIRR)

• **Can I still work on sor**

He told me last night that
him to make him feel "love"

I would suggest having a
you need to cut and clear the
person. Sometimes when a pe
answer and, in my experience

• Is there a "remove the fear" or "remove the doubt" spell?

I need help with an ex who ends relationships out of fear and now he's ended one with me. As soon as there is the slightest problem, he goes running. He told me he was afraid he'd get hurt.
— Beach

Well, as we know, relationships are full of ups and downs ... and hurt and pain are part of the course. Have you had a reading to find out what is really going on with your friend? Crucible of Courage comes to mind, as it gives a person courage in situations like this.

As for past hurts, consider Hindu Grass Oil to clean away old messes and cut ties with past events, and Reconciliation Oil to forgive and forget past problems and for a couple to fall in love again. Either can be used as an oil or candle spell. Healing Oil is another great product to mend emotional problems (physically, spiritually and emotionally. You might consider some cleansing and healing for yourself during this process.
— jwmcclin (M)

• How do I get him to leave his current relationship?

How do i get the man i love to come to me and leave his relationship that he truly doesn't want to be in?
— truelove69

Sounds like you need to break him up from his current partner, for which you would use Break Up products. You could use Come To Me, Love Me, or any of the love drawing products to bring him to you. Now, in addition to those things, you may want to get a reading from one of the reputable readers at AIRR. Although other psychics have told you
 is your "soul mate" — whenever you are about to do break up work,
 od to get a second opinion and confirm that nothing else stands in
 of you and him. Typically when people are in relationships —
 they don't want to be and sometimes especially when they
  e — there is more to the story, and you want to make sure
 bases covered.
— Miss Bri (M, AIRR)

• **What if he says, "I love you, but I'm not in love with you"?**

"He loves me but is not in love with me." Will menstrual blood change him from not in love with me to falling in love with me again?
— mabel

I've always felt the "I love you, but I'm not in love with you" line is what men say when they want to avoid commitment but keep the woman around. To me it's BS; either you love someone or you don't.
— Mama Micki (M)

Amen, sister! Like being half-pregnant — you either are, or you're not. He's using her as a back-up plan, so he's free to see what is out there.
— Literarylioness (M)

You probably need to look into WHY he doesn't find himself falling in love with you. For example, he could be afraid of getting hurt, or he could be attracted to someone else. Also, he could have someone telling him things about you OR perhaps it could be something YOU are doing.

Fix the issues you are having before you continue to do anything that is geared towards commitment. If living in different states is an issue, then I would definitely consider doing something about it. Obviously proximity is an issue for him. If he can't see you and be with you every day, then it is probably easier for him to forget about you or not feel committed to you. Sleeping with a man does not guarantee he will fall in love with you. Not saying it does not happen, but it might just create him being physically attracted to you; you might not have his heart.

I would use a skull candle here, and get into his mind. I would use some love products to dress the skull, some Follow Me Boy, some Influence, and some Licorice Root to change his mind. I would perform that spell over at least 7 nights, when he is sleeping.

I would recommend dressing the candle with menstrual blood. I say that you should do this over 7 nights because its like trying to convince someone to do something you really want them to do. If you hammer at them over a number of days versus just one day, then you probably will get through to them. It just reinforces the spell.
— starsinthesky7 (M)

• How do I calm an angry lover?

My boyfriend was very angry with me before he left. I would like any help on how can I calm his anger, and make both of us forgive.
— skyme714

You can work a blue candle on his picture anointed with Healing and Tranquility Oils to calm his anger towards you. One of the methods I've used to soothe angry people is to work with a white skull candle that's been baptised. I petition for healing as I dip my hands in a glass filled with ice to get my fingers cold and wet, then I lightly massage the skull candle as I whisper soothing words to it. This works really well to calm down temper flares. From there anoint it with your Tranquility Oil, Healing Oil, and dust it with powdered herbs like Althea and Sage.
— ConjureMan Ali (M, AIRR)

• How do I create obsession so that he will love me again?

When choosing a love spell for someone you want to love you again but also want it to be an obsession, how do you go about doing that? I want love, passion, bewitching and control.
— southern

Bewitching will give you allure and fascination — which should mean you can dial back on the controlling elements. Better a willing follower than a slave, right? Wouldn't you rather be her Favourite of All Things, rather than an addiction that makes her helpless?

To my mind, domination work is best used on men and women who will stray, cheat, desert their families, and just generally make folks miserable if they aren't kept in hand.

If you used Controlling or Bend Over or I Dominate My Woman products exclusively, without sweetening, without Chuparrosa or Blessing or any "Golden Rule" elements, then yes, your lover would resent you even if she stayed with you. The Intranquil Spirit is notorious for bringing a lover back in a mean state of mind.

In love work, my motto is: "Don't dominate. Fascinate."
— MissMichaele (M, AIRR)

• How do I gauge how my reconciliation work is going?

Shortly after I met with my rootworker, my ex contacted me.

We met a few times, he was very affectionate, and he told me how much he cares for me. We spent hours reminiscing, and on and on.

I pretty strongly hinted at a reconciliation in both my words and actions and that's when my ex felt the need to spell out for me that we are just friends now.

Unfortunately, now that he knows my intention is reconciliation, he is also taking a step back from this friendship.

Is this my completion? I was wondering, because he stands firm at friendship without much indication it could turn back into anything more.
— Babybio / Transformer

Speak with your rootworker, and see if things are still in progress. It seems you got some movement but not completion. Reconciliation work should be steady and not fast. The work needs to build a strong foundation rather than "let's get back together," sweep things under the rug, and then the same problems surface … same cycle on repeat.
— starsinthesky7 (M)

I'd say what you have seen is "movement," but not "completion." The two of you were not talking at all, now you are talking. That's movement in the right direction, but he says he wants to remain friends, and not to resume being lovers — hence this is not yet completion.

This question comes up often enough that i want to make sure that everyone gets it straight. "Completion" of your work does not mean "the spell ran out of steam." It means "I got what i wanted." And, no, you did not get what you wanted.

You two were not speaking. You did a spell for reconciliation.

You got a sign — he contacted you.

You got movement — he spoke to you again affectionately, and he reminisced, albeit only as a friend.

You did not get completion — he did not reconcile with you.

So either the spell has failed or that was movement. It was certainly not completion, unless you choose to stop there of your own accord.
— catherineyronwode (M, AIRR)

• Should I give up?

My guy and I broke up so I did several spells to draw him back: I rolled his sock toward me, started a sugar jar with a white candle, and cleaned house with Chinese Wash. He came back the next day to apologize, and we made love, but he is staying at his mother's and refuses to move back in. He says he wants to be "friends with benefits." I told him that will not do, either come back or stay away, and he got angry. I feel like I have ruined everything. I got my sign and I got definite movement, but I don't know now if I can actually complete the spell as I had hoped. Should I give up?
— blackberry

When you are getting movement like this, and the person reaches out to you after you've done reconciliation work or are in the middle of it, I think it is important to not force things or let them know your intentions straight out. Take the time to ease back into things rather than rush it. And you surely do not want to rush back into something without changing previous behaviours. Otherwise, it's just going to be the same thing all over again, with the same bad outcome.

Accept and listen to what he is saying. I would rather have close proximity to the target as a friend, which can always progress, than unleash all my feelings about how I want to reconcile, so he gets freaked out and runs away. This is not productive to the work, and can set the process back.
— starsinthesky7 (M)

You got great signs and very swift movement, but you crossed up your own work by tipping your hand too soon. I would not give up, though. I would add some further spells to "carry the good work on." Try some binding spells now, the kind that are hidden in the bed, applied through laundering the sheets, tying knots in a semen-soaked string and carrying it on you, or feeding him your sexual fluids.

I would not give up unless the spell does not reach a satisfactory completion within three months. Only then — unless i had deliberately and aforehandedly set a longer time limit (such as "a year and a day," or "until my next birthday" or such) — would i consider it to have failed and after that i would either try another approach or give up the case.
— catherineyronwode (M, AIRR)

• He said horrible, contradictory things, what do I do?

He said some downright horrible things — I think mostly just to hurt me and to try to get me to finally give up on him. It would be easier if I could believe he meant all those things, but he said things that were contradictory and I can't wrap my head around them. I am desperate.
— Jess-Belle

When a person gets that down and dirty, more often then not he was being truthful. You point out "contradictions" but those are your "what if" to hold on to him and hope things work out.

You can do lots of work but I can tell you this: being desperate, begging, pleading, over thinking, over trying, stalking, texting, calling, apologizing has never brought a man back.

You are making excuses to hold on, and once upon a time I did the same: what if he meant it this way, what if he meant it that way, but he texts me, but he was mad at me and mad is an emotion so he cares. I have been there with the wrong person, holding on with a death grip, trying anything to get them back out of fear of not being loved. Thinking this was my chance and I messed it up and now it's lost — all lies by the Devil.

Truth, you will heal. You will move on and will meet someone better, but, hun, you need to start to believe that too. Do a Cut and Clear spell, and then do a new working when ready to draw a new love.
— j82

• What can I do besides Cut and Clear?

Is there anything I can use besides Cut and Clear to remove feelings for someone? Will it make two people stop loving one another?
— Wanttounderstand

Cut and Clear is used on yourself — it is notused to break up people. You could start with Black Walnuts to rid yourself of feelings for your ex, then Cut and Clear and Road Opening to open new avenues in love. Crucible of Courage can give you strength to do what needs to be done. You could use Healing Oil to heal any emotional wounds that there may be.
— Devi Spring (M, AIRR)

• He cheated and we are both angry; how can we get along?

I want to get along with my boyfriend, but we fight all of the time, and not just normal couples-fighting; I'm talking cussing, telling each other I hate you, and getting so angry at each other that we broke up. I want to stop him from going back to the girl he cheated on me with, but I also want to stop letting him stress me out. I am a little afraid of trying a spell and it backfiring on me. Any ideas?

— Wanttounderstand

First off, let me address the issue of spells "backfiring." Spells are not supposed to backfire. If they do, that means you're either not carrying them out right, or you're wrecking the spell's intention and energy by obsessing over it after casting it. Don't carry out a love spell, and every day think to yourself, "Oh, my spells are always backfiring. I'm sure this one will too. Oh, I'm no good at casting spells. Will it work this time?" You must be confident in your abilities and your work, otherwise doing any spell at all would just be a waste of money, time and energy.

Okay, now to move on to your problems! I'm sorry to say there isn't one single spell or product that can fix all your problems. You have to do several separate spells, one step at a time, to help with your situation.

First of all, you have to decide whether you still want to be with this man. How do you feel about him? Do you still love him? Does he love you? If not, you should not even do the work.

For quarrels and arguments: A honey or sugar jar will help sweeten the relationship and how both of you see and treat each other.

For his cheating on you: I would Hot Foot the other girl or do a freezer spell to ensure he doesn't see her again. You could also get a nation sack made, and tie up his nature to prevent him from being able to perform with other women. Also look into Commanding, Compelling, and I Dominate My Man products to make him more "obeying."

To make him realise what he's done: Clarity products would work wonders, along with King Solomon Wisdom and Healing products.

To forgive him: A mix of Healing, Love Me, and Reconciliation would help. Dress the house with Peace Water. Put Peaceful Home bath crystals in the laundry for his clothes as well as for your towels and bed-linens.

— Annabelle / silver_disc

• **I was caught cheating. How do we reconcile?**

My girlfriend went through my phone and found a text from another woman. How can I reconcile and move on from where we left off?
— Grantmojo

Well, the first thing to do is to apologize, apologize, apologize. Healing, Reconciliation, and Return to Me are all good formulas to use in situations like this. I also recommend a frank, open, and honest conversation with her (and yourself) about why you were texting the other woman and what it might mean about your current relationship.
— Miss Bri (M, AIRR)

• **He found out I was cheating, now he only wants me for sex.**

He found out about me and my friend being physical and got mad. I made a honey jar with red candles, dressed with Return To Me. He did return, and says he is still interested, but he became abusive and now he only wants me for purely physical aspects. Should I continue the honey jar, but now dress it with the Love Me and Stay With Me oils? Also, should I begin using pink candles instead of red, for more romantic interest?
— Tzigana

There must be a certain respect given to destiny and fate. Some things simply aren't "meant to be," however as conjure-workers we understand that destiny is in our hands and if we are determined enough to do something, then we shouldn't let anything stop us. You can use magic to bring this guy to you, but it might not be as happy or fulfilling as you expected. Despite that, if you seek to continue, then here is my advice:

Keep working with the honey jar. Keep him sweet to you. Do not cut off the sex. Dress red candles with Love Me or Stay With Me Oil. You can also sexually charge a red penis candle with his name on it and fix it with your sexual fluids mixed with the oils and burn it on his picture or name paper. If you want to draw him closer, then work a moving Lodestone love spell over a period of seven days. Finally, feed him some of your menstrual blood to really bond him to you. Hope that helps.
— ConjureMan Ali (M, AIRR)

• How do I successfully begin and end the reconciliation process?

Me and my ex broke up three months ago. If i do a love spell now to get her back, would i have faster results than if i wait a year or two?
— freddy

Typically reconciliation spell work is more successful if it is performed BEFORE it gets to the point of a break up.

If you are broken up already, then you'll want to do reconciliation work ASAP. The longer you wait, the less likely you'll be successful. Additionally, you really want to have an open line of good communication between the two of you (no, not just text messages! lol). And you'll want closer proximity to one another for best results.

Just remember that reconciliation work is very iffy, and depends on a LOT of factors, including the emotional state of both people involved, the reasons for the break up, whether the ex has a new partner, etc.

In your case, after three months, this is something you should really get a reading on, in order to determine if your chances are good, and what route of action to take. Just keep in mind, it will take a lot of energy and a slow steady progress in terms of magic. You won't flip a switch and get that person back in two seconds.
— Dr. E. (M, AIRR)

Start the love-return spells now. Don't wait. Back up your spiritual work by actions that actually support the desire for reconciliation. If you are doing sweet and drawing spells but bringing up past issues or talking about problems, that isn't helping to further the sweetening. If you feel that these old issues need addressing, then add some soothing Balm of Gilead to your conjure and have an all-out discussion about what you are feeling. Get it all out on the table, then move on and start fresh.
— ConjureMan Ali (M, AIRR)

I always tell my clients to start at once, and when the target returns, to change their course of action to Stay With Me spells. You do this as soon as the ex comes back and continue to do it while the relationship is stable.

It's kind of like "preventative medicine"!
— Miss Aida (M, AIRR)